ABOUT THE AUTHOR

Nazir Afzal OBE is former a Chief Crown Prosecutor and was Chief Executive of the UK's Police and Crime Commissioners. During a 24-year career, Nazir prosecuted some of the most high profile cases in the country and advised on many others, with a special focus on domestic violence, child sexual abuse, and honour-based violence. He worked personally on the most high-profile cases whilst simultaneously overseeing the thousands of prosecutions each year, and is particularly known for his prosecution of the so-called Rochdale sex grooming gang. Today he sits on the board of the Independent Press Standards Organisation (IPSO) and is also National Adviser on Gender Based Violence to the Welsh Government. In 2018 he joined the advisory board of Google's Innovation Fund for counter-extremism.

THE
PROSECUTOR

NAZIR AFZAL

THE PROSECUTOR

One Man's Pursuit of Justice for the Voiceless

EBURY
PRESS

1

Ebury Press, an imprint of Ebury Publishing,
20 Vauxhall Bridge Road,
London SW1V 2SA

Ebury Press is part of the Penguin Random House group of companies
whose addresses can be found at global.penguinrandomhouse.com

Penguin
Random House
UK

First published by Ebury Press in 2020
This edition published by Ebury Press in 2021

www.penguin.co.uk

A CIP catalogue record for this book is available from the British Library

ISBN 9781529105025

Printed and bound in Great Britain by Clays Ltd, Elcograf S.p.A.

The authorized representative in the EEA is Penguin Random House
Ireland, Morrison Chambers, 32 Nassau Street, Dublin D02 YH68

Penguin Random House is committed to a sustainable
future for our business, our readers and our planet. This book
is made from Forest Stewardship Council® certified paper.

To our children

Prologue

The sweltering heat is what I remember most. It was 1976, one of the hottest years on record, and that day the sun beat down particularly fiercely on Birmingham. The air on Hobmoor Road shimmered like burning paraffin. I was on my way home from school and had stopped to take advantage of some shade, wiping the sweat from my forehead, when I heard the shout from across the road.

'Oi, Paki, hold up!'

I stiffened and looked up, seeing three boys across the street. They were quickening their stride and heading towards me. They were bigger and older than me, probably at least sixteen. I was only thirteen but, with enough experience to recognise the threat they posed, my body took over. I felt the adrenaline surge straight to my feet.

Without looking back, I began running as fast as I could in the opposite direction.

My arms and legs pumping furiously, I tore along the pavement. Looking frantically for an escape route, I cut across the road diagonally, darting towards a side street. I dared to look back – and they were gaining on me.

But as I turned, I skidded. A cyclist was coming straight towards me and, dodging out of the way, I tripped on the kerb, rolling onto the pavement. They were upon me in a flash. A flurry of punches knocked me to the floor, the metallic taste of blood immediately filling my mouth. I curled myself into the foetal position, clutching my head with my hands as all three of them began booting, stamping, attacking me in a frenzy.

What saved me was a minicab, screeching to a stop in front of us and blasting its horn. As the three of them fled, the taxi driver jumped from the car and ran to my side.

'You OK?' he asked, helping to lift me. My ankle was badly twisted, and my face was swelling so quickly that already I couldn't see out of one eye.

He whistled and shook his head.

'They've sure done a job on you,' he said. He offered to drive me home.

When I got there, it was Dad who opened the door. There was shock in his eyes as he pulled me inside. He held onto me for a minute, studying the bruising on my face. 'Don't let your mum see you like this,' he said, as he guided me upstairs to the bathroom.

He was silent as he washed my cuts and bandaged my head to stop the bleeding, dabbing at my face with a foul-smelling antiseptic cream. He didn't need to say anything. He knew.

'They shouldn't get away with this,' I said, finally. I wanted to go to the police, I told him. I knew what they looked like, and I knew they were breaking the law. He furrowed his brow as I spoke.

'I want justice,' I said.

Dad sighed. I'd heard that sigh before. He seemed exhausted. 'That's a lot of big talk,' he said slowly. 'The law. Justice. Police. What do you honestly think will happen, Nazir?'

I didn't know how to answer him.

'The police are not interested in you,' he said, softly. 'They don't care about us. Justice doesn't mean anything to us. Just make sure you don't walk home alone from school next time.' He dabbed away at my face. 'Stay one step ahead of them, right? Because there is no justice.'

I wanted to challenge him, to tell him that he was wrong, but I couldn't. My mouth seemed to be on strike.

There is no justice.

Maybe he was right. And maybe, deep down, I knew it too. It wasn't the first time this kind of thing had happened, and I certainly wasn't the only person in my community to be attacked for the colour of my skin. The blows kept coming. Why now did I suddenly think the law could help me? Whenever I caught the ball in rugby at school, kids would shout, 'Get the Paki!', slam me to the ground and grind my face in the mud. And every time, I had kept quiet. When a group of boys at school ripped the sleeve off my new school jacket, I'd not only held my tongue but did my best to hide the evidence from Mum. I raided her sewing kit and inexpertly sewed the sleeve back on. I didn't want my parents to know what was happening to me, and I certainly didn't want them to think that I couldn't handle the abuse I was getting. Even if they probably knew all along.

But this time, I had realised something. Racism wasn't a test I had to pass. It wasn't something I had to put up with. And I certainly wasn't going to spend the rest of my life running from abusers.

'There, all done,' Dad said, taping a gauze patch above my eyebrow. 'Get some sleep and don't think about them. They're not worth it.'

Later, when Dad came in to say goodnight, I asked if he could leave the hall light on. I couldn't sleep that night, and its soft glow crept under my door. I stared at the ceiling, wide-eyed, the warm breeze floating through the open window along with the muted sounds of the neighbourhood. Dad's words rattled around my mind.

There is no justice.

I tossed and turned in my sheets. But peace wouldn't come. I lay for hours, my mind racing. And I waited for daybreak.

I

It might not have seemed like it that afternoon, but Dad hadn't always been so sceptical about the idea of justice. In fact, it was the reason that he brought us to England in the first place, and it was he who instilled in me from an early age the importance of doing your best to right a wrong.

Muhammad, or 'Baba' as we called him, worked for many years as a caterer in the British army. Born in what is now Pakistan, as part of his service to the British he had been stationed in India, first throughout the Second World War and then for decades afterwards. In 1960, he was offered the chance to work at a military base in Cyprus. Not long after he arrived, he was robbed of a sizeable sum of money. Under a hot sun in a tent in Akrotiri, he vowed to find the thief and recover what was owed.

Anyone who served in the British army at the time would have known not to mess with the caterers. Char Wallahs had a history of pursuing people across the globe if they didn't settle their 'tick' book, and Dad was no exception. It took him less than year to find out who was responsible and that they were now in England. Never one to hang around, he boarded a plane to Heathrow.

It was the beginning of the swinging sixties and London was at its heart. Dad was in no rush to return home, so while he sought out his money, he chose to stay a while and explore the city.

Staying in a bedsit in West London with fellow immigrants, Dad was soon in demand for his skills with the English language. It wasn't long before his neighbours relied on him to translate for them – and I bet those same people played a part in helping my dad get his stolen money back. Because in not much time at all, he had tracked down the thief and recovered his money (nobody was hurt in the process, I'm assured by my mum).

Dad, with his reinstated wealth, looked around him and began to wonder, *Could this be home?* There was something about the spirit of the city that appealed to him, and within weeks he had invited his wife and sons, my brothers, to join him. It was easier to emigrate back then and, being a member of the Commonwealth, Pakistanis were almost encouraged to come to Britain to help ease labour shortages.

The family settled in Ealing first, but found it isolated, and Dad soon tracked down a distant relative in Birmingham, discovering that a few new arrivals from villages near ours in Pakistan had also begun to settle in the Midlands. Dad thought that as he was moving with his wife and kids, he needed to be close to others like him. Support and protection – the things offered by a community – were uppermost in his mind.

Plenty of work of a menial nature was to be found in the industrial heartlands, and Dad immediately got a job in a factory making metal goods and building materials. He had his savings, along with an income of £7 a week and a roof of his own over his head. There was a world of opportunity before him. In England, he saw schools teaching kids for free. When he was sick, he could see a doctor for free, and receive medication for free. What was not to like? Well, OK, there were the skinheads on the street telling him to 'go home' – but once he closed his front door, they were outside, he was indoors. The decision was made. This was going to be our home.

A year later, in October 1962, I was born. What we lacked in space, in that cramped terraced house, we more than made up for in love. They say home isn't a place, it's a feeling, and in those four walls I always felt safe and loved.

My earliest memories of Birmingham are of its inner-city bustle. The crowds of people shopping, the double-decker buses lining the streets, everyone rushing to get somewhere. We were one of the first Asian families to settle there, along with Dad's relatives. Living near to the football ground, we could often hear the clamour of fans on their way to St Andrew's and later in the afternoon, the sounds of the terrace chants. I didn't understand what the fans were singing and even though the sounds could be joyful, their volume made me anxious.

Birmingham City were a major force back then. They were the first English club side to take part in European competition and in 1963 they won the League Cup. Years later, as I grew up, I learned to avoid football fans, knowing that the cruellest taunts – and the biggest risk of violence – often came from them. As a small child, though, I would gawp with fascination at them, dressed in their club colours and marching down the street in the haze of noise and excitement.

The only memory as vivid as all that is of my first day at Marlborough Infant School. I stood alone in the playground, tears tumbling down my cheeks as I cried out for my mum. I adored her. My dad was a man of justice, but Mum was always the backbone of the family; I can't remember a time when she wasn't there for us. She had never left her village in Pakistan before she came to England, but when she arrived, she blossomed. She adapted so quickly to her new world and seized its opportunities.

We saw less of Dad, as he was forever working. It was rare to come in and see his jacket hanging on the bannister. But when he was home, he was frequently accompanied by strangers and our front room would become the setting for lively meetings. He was building a network, working hard to become the voice of an emerging Pakistani community in Birmingham. He thought that together, we would be stronger. He was driven by a need to help people: If someone needed something, he would be there.

Dad had always thought it was individuals that changed the world, not bureaucracy. He didn't believe in institutions or government and he didn't trust the authorities. The police walked by when we were attacked, so we certainly couldn't trust them to keep us safe. Coming from a country where the government was riddled with corruption, he knew he couldn't rely on the state to solve anything, let alone everything.

He could see there was a gap at the heart of our society. The community around us didn't trust the authorities and needed someone to speak on their behalf. Dad believed passionately in civil society, in the idea that people were at the heart of change, and wanted to fill this gap – so our house became a kind of citizens advice bureau. It was a powerful lesson for me: from an early age I saw how small groups of people working together could make a difference.

Throughout my childhood, people would come to the house night and day seeking Dad's counsel. They might want him to write a letter on their behalf to the local council about some matter, or give them his help to get their deceased relatives back to Pakistan for burial. Whatever the request, he would never say no. As his skills became known in the community, demand for his help grew, and it wasn't long before I was his secretary, writing and sending out dozens of letters a week on behalf of our neighbours. I would come home from school wanting to watch cartoons or play with toys, and Dad would step into my room and clear his throat.

'I have some letters for you to write,' he would say.

And I would spend the next few hours sat on the settee with a notepad on my knee, taking on local people's problems and trying to get things done for our community.

Not a lot came from those letters, in all honesty. However, they still had an important role to play: because of them, people knew that their views had been made known, that someone was working on their behalf. When we worked together, we didn't always have power, but we did have a voice.

Sometimes, though, we did get results. I remember one man who was in a lot of pain visiting my dad. He had been waiting six months for a sinus operation and begged us to write to the hospital for him. He was in agony. So, Dad dictated a letter and I sat on the settee hurriedly writing (using big words for a ten-year-old) how this delay was causing the man serious consequences, asking for the situation to be remedied at the earliest available opportunity. Within only a few weeks, the necessary operation had been performed. Miraculously, the problem had been solved almost immediately. The man was elated, and it was an important moment for us too. After all, this was the early 1970s. There was no one and nowhere to turn to for help. No *Watchdog*, no Inspectorate. Nothing.

By 1968, Dad's reputation preceded him, and his efforts to support the local community had grown to the extent that they could no longer be run from our living room. His work needed more structure, so Dad established the first immigrant organisation in Birmingham: the Pak Pakhtoon Association. Using funds collected by the community, a small property was purchased where people could meet and organise. The Association has since celebrated its fiftieth anniversary and today has over 10,000 members, representing all walks of life and professions from taxi drivers and labourers to doctors and pilots.

While Dad was busy either earning money for our family or working with the community, it was Mum that we all continued to count on. And with six sons, four of whom were under ten, and a baby girl, our home – a three-bedroomed terrace with an outside toilet – was chaotic at times. She would even breastfeed on the stairs, which was sometimes the only peaceful spot in our frenetic home. But it was a happy household, full of laughter, love and music.

Mum was also actively involved in the community. I didn't understand it at the time, but Dad relied on her to encourage the women of the community to get involved with the Pak Pakhtoon Association, and she spent much of her time fighting on a different front, for the rights of the women at home. Being responsible for feeding and clothing everyone, keeping the home clean and liveable, all on a few pounds a week and with no visible support, Mum was all too aware of the hardships that women could face. She understood that dozens of other women were alone while their husbands worked to put food on the table and were struggling, often having moved thousands of miles from home and from their family. But

Mum, like Dad, believed they could build a new community here. After all, these women were all within walking distance of our home. And so she would often take us all to see them. With me, two baby brothers and a baby sister in the pram or strapped to her side, she would stride into their homes, often without so much as even a knock on the door or an invitation, to check on them while their husbands were out. The visits weren't just about making sure everyone was coping. Mum did much more than that. In one kitchen one afternoon, a neighbour told her that she had a fourteen-year-old daughter she was planning to marry off to a cousin in Pakistan. We watched as Mum argued animatedly.

'You can't do that! She's far too young. What on earth are you thinking?' she demanded, shaking her head. She told the woman not to bow to any pressure from Pakistan. 'You need this girl here,' she said. Lowering her voice, she added that it was against Islam to force a woman to marry.

In kitchens across Small Heath, Mum would wear women down like this. Once she knew the argument was won, she'd smile and put the kettle on. She was a force of nature.

'Just think about the chances she has here,' Mum would conclude, as she poured the tea. 'She can work, she can study.' She knew that, back in Pakistan, these opportunities were not easily available, and she believed wholeheartedly that education was the way to liberate girls.

My mum was fourteen when she married my dad, who himself was only sixteen. I wondered if that had been on her mind all those years, and contributed to her becoming such a tireless fighter for other girls. My parents seemed very happy together, but those kitchen confrontations about the rights of girls to have their freedom stayed in my mind. Years later, when I helped to make forced marriage become a crime, I would think back to those days, marvelling at how Mum had been such a pioneer and how I had, at the time, taken it rather for granted.

My mind was probably on simpler things. We had just got our first television, and we were beside ourselves with excitement, crowding around the black and white screen and fiddling with the knobs until we got the picture perfect. From our front room we were suddenly connected to the world. We all sat in silence watching the first landing on the moon in 1969, eyes agog as the lunar module descended and Neil Armstrong climbed down the ladder.

My memories of that time are warmed by the feeling of security that a tight-knit family brings. But there were other feelings too. Even though Mum was so confident in her family and community, I knew she didn't trust many people outside of that core group. That was why I had been born at home, because she didn't trust hospitals. And I knew my dad was unsettled by the hostilities often experienced by our community.

We often felt we were only visitors in England and there was an unspoken understanding that without any warning, we might be told to leave. This, I later discovered, was why Dad worked so hard, saving as much money as possible to take us back to Pakistan if and when the time came.

This became increasingly clear to me as I grew up, especially when I first expressed an interest in studying law. 'No, no, no,' Dad would sigh, exasperated. 'We don't need lawyers in Pakistan. There's lots of them, and they're all corrupt. You need to study to be a doctor or an engineer. That's what Pakistan needs.'

It came as no real surprise when in the winter of 1969 Dad announced that we were going back to Pakistan, if only for a six-month trip. It was for my eldest brother Umar's arranged marriage but it was also the first time I would visit Pakistan – and I suspect Dad wanted to give us a taste of where our future might lie if we were forced out of Britain.

Not a man to do things by halves, my dad somehow got hold of a twelve-seater white Ford transit van to take us all the way from Dover to Pakistan.

It had taken Aldrin and Armstrong four days to get to the moon but it was going to take us a whole lot longer to get to North West Pakistan. Indeed, to me, the distance to travel felt about the same: almost a month of hard road lay ahead of us. As the van shifted into gear and jolted forward off the ferry in Belgium, none of us knew what to expect.

At first, the thrill of adventure kept everyone in good spirits. It was crowded in the back with my mum, my brothers and sister, my six-year-old cousin Yasmin and me. We huddled together to stay warm when the temperature dropped, and

Mum had a small cooking stove with a few pans that she used to keep us all fed. Through the Belgian countryside and on towards Germany we raced, playing games, singing and laughing, as Dad gripped the wheel and concentrated doggedly on the road ahead, keeping his foot pressed to the floor.

I watched the roads flash by and looked towards the German mountains and forests covered in snow. I spent the rest of the time talking to Yasmin. She was mixed race, with white skin, dark hair and beautiful brown eyes. Yasmin had come along with us because she was the firstborn of my uncle and his Irish wife, and they wanted her to see Pakistan. She also liked spending time with us and was particularly close to Mum and me. We were roughly the same age, but she had more confidence and quite the mischievous streak. Her smile alone was always enough to make me feel better, and I was over the moon that she had joined us.

Mum, on the other hand, was finding it less fun. She spent a lot of time in the back of the van praying, and though she said little, I knew she wasn't impressed at having to drive through Europe in winter. As she protectively wrapped a blanket round my sister when the temperature dropped, I could see an angry glint in her eye.

Onwards we drove, through Germany and Austria to Yugoslavia where Mum's mood darkened as Dad's driving became increasingly erratic, beginning to put us in danger. The roads had been deteriorating as the miles passed, tarmac giving way to loose gravel and eventually becoming almost unpassable dirt roads. Dad, however, continued to plough on as though he was driving down the motorway, even on dangerous hairpin bends. Any apologies he made had little effect on Mum, who at one point refused to talk for what felt like days in silent protest.

As we drove through Greece the mood brightened a little, and Dad came alive with stories. He'd always believed he had some Greek blood and we smiled as he began to regale us with stories of Alexander the Great's conquering armies. He told us how they had established outposts in the North West Frontier Province of Pakistan during the time of Alexander's conquests, so that many now claimed to be descendants of Alexander the Great's troops. Perhaps, I thought we might be too.

I usually loved hearing Dad's stories, but now weariness descended upon us and we drove through Turkey, Iran and Afghanistan mostly in silence, the countries and days blurring together. I was desperate to sleep in a proper bed again. Finally, at the end of December, we crossed the Afghanistan border and arrived in the North West Frontier Province in Pakistan. After three and a half gruelling weeks, the van finally juddered to a halt at the bottom of a dirt path leading to my parents' home village of Saleh Khana.

The name Saleh Khana derives from the Arabic, meaning 'home of the good people', and it more than lived up to its name. The welcome we received was rapturous, with dozens of members of our extended family – none of whom I'd ever met before – materialising on the path to greet us, staring at our dusty vehicle as though it had come straight off the set of a movie. There were no cars or vans in the village, only buses.

Our family home had been locked up for eight years, and was a very different proposition to our house in Birmingham. This one may not have had running water, but it did have large bedrooms and plenty of space and after being cooped up in a van for such a long time, it felt like the Ritz. But there was no time yet to catch up on lost sleep. There were people to meet, adventures to be had, and everywhere we went, people wanted to know about our life in England.

I spent the next five and a half months playing outside, eating at different houses, diving in water pools and fishing. Yasmin was my constant companion as we ran from one house and excitement to the next. As we watched the sunset over the high Cherat mountains one evening, my family alongside our new friends and extended family, I started to understand the sense of community that Dad talked about, and why he had been so keen to recreate a version of it in England.

There were other surprises too. One afternoon I saw a group of boys walking up the hill with large bowls of curry, rice and fruit, staggering slightly under their weight.

'Where are they taking that?' I asked a cousin, who was playing with me in the courtyard at the time.

'To the hippies,' he said, pointing to a big white house on the hill.

'Who are the hippies?' I asked.

'Go and see for yourself,' he laughed mischievously. 'If you run, you can catch them.'

I ran after the boys, Yasmin at my side as usual, and asked if we could join them. As we approached the hippies' house, strange music floated from the windows on the afternoon breeze. It didn't sound like anything Mum or Dad would listen to. It was, in fact, the Doors – and Jim Morrison's rich baritone urged us to break on through to the other side.

We knocked on the door and it was opened by a young blonde woman, wearing a floral print kaftan and patchwork leather hat. She beckoned us in with a smile, and we followed her into the kitchen where half a dozen skinny white folk sat hunched over what looked like a glass pipe. A cloud of smoke hovered despite the open windows and my eyes watered. The smell was terrible.

'Food!' exclaimed a long-haired man with a headband and lurid tie-dye T-shirt, leaping up from his chair. 'Get the plates, Tina.'

Suddenly, the group huddled round the table came to life. Plates, cutlery and drinks rapidly appeared, and we were handed glasses of orange squash. We had barely sat down before they started hungrily devouring our offerings, shovelling away the curry and rice as though they were starving. I'd never seen anyone eat that way. They must be terribly poor, I thought.

We perched on a large red beanbag and watched the scene before us with fascination. Yasmin sipped her orange squash and we exchanged awkward glances. Other than my teachers back in England, I hadn't spent much time with white people, and these guys were unlike anyone I'd encountered before.

'I see we've got new recruits,' Tina said with a smile, looking at Yasmin and me. 'What are your names?' We nervously introduced ourselves and a man at the table asked if we liked music.

I nodded.

'Then pin your ears back and get a load of this,' he said, slipping some vinyl onto a turntable and dropping the needle.

For a few moments all we could hear was a strange crackle. Then the stylus found the grooves and we listened as the wah-wah opening of Jimi Hendrix's 'Voodoo Chile' exploded into full sonic force. When I heard it years later, back in the UK, I would be transported to that strange afternoon.

Tina closed her eyes and began to dance, swaying hypnotically at first then waving her arms like a strange windmill. Yasmin nudged me. The bemused look in her eyes suggested it was time to go.

'We'd better get back to our parents,' I said, struggling to make myself heard over the music.

The man with the long hair and the headband grinned.

'You'll appreciate it more when you're older. See you tomorrow.'

After we'd parted company with the other boys at the bottom of the hill, Yasmin and I went to see Dad and told him about the hippies.

'Why take food to that house?' I asked. He rubbed his stubble, chuckled and sat us both down.

'Islam is not just about going to the mosque, you know, it's a way of life. And if you have a visitor, you feed them. Hospitality is a right, not a gift.'

In Pakistan, there was far more to learn than I'd ever learned at school, every day bringing rich new experiences. Some of these were more dangerous than others. One afternoon, we were in the courtyard playing when Mum dashed out of the house and told us to get inside immediately. She spoke with a panic we had rarely heard before so for once, we all did as we were told.

She took us upstairs and opened a large wardrobe in one of the bedrooms. 'Get in,' she said. 'Don't worry,' she told Yasmin, two of my brothers and younger sister and me, as she locked the door behind us. 'You'll be safe here. Wait until I come and get you.'

A dispute over some land had taken a violent turn, and debate had escalated into fierce conflict. It would appear that people didn't go to court here; scores were settled differently. We pulled each other close in the wardrobe and waited, hearing the dull sounds of glass smashing, wood splintering. But we could always trust Mum: eventually she came to get us, and we were safe again.

Spring arrived. White poppies, jasmines and carnations flowered in the fields, and the day of my eldest brother Umar's wedding came.

The celebration went on for days. I'd never experienced anything like it: the singing and dancing, the flowers and ribbons everywhere, row after row of tables groaning under huge plates of sumptuous food. Even the hippies came down to join us, and Yasmin and I danced the night away. The celebrations went on into the early hours, and we were so exhausted that Dad picked the pair of us up and threw us over his shoulder. We were both asleep before he had even reached the stairs. It was one of the happiest times of my life.

But it wasn't to last. Soon afterwards, Dad announced it was time to return to the UK. We had to get back in time for school, which was starting in autumn.

There were so many goodbyes to say. Yet while I was upset to be leaving, part of me was happy to be going back to Birmingham, to return to my old life. Before we went, though, there was one last chance to visit the hippies.

They seemed genuinely saddened when we told them we would be leaving in the morning. The man with the long hair and the headband who had introduced us to Jimi Hendrix had grown a moustache now and resembled George Harrison. He appeared lost in thought, then started rummaging around the front room. 'Let me get you something,' he mumbled. 'A token of thanks.'

He presented me with a silver pendant on a leather cord necklace. It had a strange logo, which looked like a circle divided into four uneven segments. 'CND, man,' he said. 'It'll bring you good vibes.'

Yasmin was presented with a flower headband by Tina, who insisted we listen to some songs from a new Beatles album before we left. We lay on the red beanbag listening to 'Across the Universe', 'Let it Be' and Tina's favourite, 'The Long and Winding Road'.

I began thinking of the winding roads in Yugoslavia we'd soon have to navigate again. Particularly those hairpin bends.

The next day we set off. The sun was only just beginning to rise over Peshawar when Dad woke us in the early hours. He was eager to get on the road, throwing our bags into the back of the van as Mum closed up the house. I could see that the determined look in his eye had returned, and it made me nervous.

He turned the keys and the engine roared into life immediately. Without even so much as a glance back, Dad accelerated down the dirt road, pebbles and dust billowing out behind us, as we headed to Afghanistan, then through Iran, then through Turkey on the journey back to Europe. The van hummed with speed, and this journey seemed much quicker than the one that had brought us to Pakistan.

Something wasn't right, however. By the time we reached Germany, Yasmin had become ill, sickness descending on her out of nowhere. Her plaintive sobs went straight to my heart, but we had no idea what was wrong with her or what to do. Mum cradled her head and tried to soothe her, Dad watching anxiously through the rear-view mirror. Very soon we would be back in England, he said, and then we could go to the doctor. We had no idea how serious things truly were.

Eventually, Yasmin seemed to ease. Her crying quietened and, in the back of the van, having her hair stroked by Mum, resting in her lap, she seemed calmer, as though she were getting better. Eventually, she stopped crying altogether, and I drifted in and out of sleep. We were close, I knew, to the port of Ostend, and that would take us back across to England.

I was jolted awake as we came to a halt at the entrance to the port. It was then that next to me, my mother stiffened, seeming almost to stop breathing.

'Nazir,' she said very softly, 'I need to speak to your father.' I looked across at Yasmin, who was completely still. She seemed to be sleeping peacefully. Mum got out of the van, and spoke to Dad in hushed tones.

What I didn't know then was that Mum had just told Dad that Yasmin had passed away beside me, her rapid sickness, as we would later learn, having given way to severe dehydration. It had taken just a matter of hours. Standing beside the van in a state of shock, they were trying to work out what to do. They decided to drive straight through to England, reporting Yasmin's death as soon as we arrived in Dover. The main priority remained to get us all home, Yasmin with us.

When Mum and Dad returned to the van I could see that Dad was shaken. He quietly assured us all we'd be home soon, but he couldn't look at Yasmin. I turned to Mum and asked her if Yasmin was alright, sensing that something was very wrong, but she insisted that Yasmin was sleeping. 'She's very ill, and in a really deep sleep,' Mum told me. 'I want you to hold her on the ferry, and look after her. If anyone asks, you just say she's sleeping.'

Mother began to pray, softly reciting scripture. I could understand bits of her prayer and I knew she was blessing Yasmin's soul. I lifted Yasmin's head and ran my hands through her beautiful dark hair, stroking her cheek. The last time I saw Yasmin, she was being carried away by an official at Dover. In the busy ferry terminal, I was crying so hard that I couldn't breathe. My mother, brothers and sister held on to each other tightly and wept bitterly, their bodies shaking with grief while Dad, having spoken to the police, rang his brother with the unbearable news.

It was late when we arrived back in Birmingham, and the moon was fading in the early morning sky. Our house looked exactly the same, but everything was different. My world had changed forever.

Yasmin was buried a few days later in Birmingham.

Soon after, I was back at school and I found that the only way I could cope with my grief was by throwing myself into my studies. Suddenly, I had a hunger to know everything about everything. Knowledge seemed to be the only answer for me – perhaps if I had known more, I would have been able to save Yasmin.

Every night I'd spend an hour after school at the mosque studying Islamic teaching, and after that, I would go to the library. Once home and my parents had gone to bed, I watched the Open University broadcasts on television, sneaking downstairs when I should have been asleep. After the programme had finished, I would end up lost in my thoughts, staring at the test-card girl playing noughts and crosses.

I didn't realise it at the time, but the pursuit of knowledge had been my way of coping with Yasmin's death, of imagining the ways I could have saved her, if only I had known how. Later, I'd feel angry, angry that my parents hadn't known how sick she was nor how to save her. As an eight-year-old, however, I felt only unbearable guilt. Yasmin had been the most vibrant girl I had ever known. She was so full of life. Why hadn't I been able to do anything to save her? Why hadn't I been powerful enough, or clever enough? Whenever I found myself alone, the same thoughts would eat me up. I felt useless and weak.

These thoughts followed me from my boyhood into my adult life. Years later in law school, I sat in lectures thinking of Yasmin. When I first became a solicitor in Birmingham, when I moved up the career ladder in London and then in Manchester, my mind went back to that eight-year-old boy unable to sleep because he couldn't get his little cousin out of his mind. Her loss has stayed with me for decades. I have come to prosecute hundreds of cases where voiceless girls have achieved justice and every time, it is as though a part of Yasmin has been present.

As a family we no longer talk about Yasmin, and her mother and father died a long time ago. Her memory lives strongly in me, however. I can still remember watching her dance at my brother's wedding, rose petals in her hair, sunlight dappled around her as she beckons me to join her. And then I feel the sea spray on my face, as I did when I got out of Dad's van at Dover. In some ways, the numbness I felt at that moment has never left me. I didn't want to be someone carrying a body: I wanted to be the person who stopped death happening in the first place. Every time I set foot in court, years later, I would think of her. Her memory would drive me to make change happen. And I was going to change things by changing myself.

II

Yasmin's death was not the only tragedy to befall our family.

After we returned to England, Dad decided that he'd had enough of factory work, and set about building a catering business called Afzal & Sons. As ever, he brought his fierce determination to his work, so it was no surprise that the fledgling business quickly became a success. In 1971, Dad tendered for a contract with a regiment he had worked for in Cyprus and this eventually got him work in Northern Ireland. By the summer of 1973, the business was thriving and my brothers and other relatives were in Northern Ireland helping the growing business.

My head, meanwhile, was buried in Harper Lee's *To Kill a Mockingbird*. I lost myself in it entirely, seeing a whole new world through the eyes of a six-year-old girl and watching Atticus Finch seek out justice. But across the Irish Sea in Derry, something brutal and all too real was about to happen.

My father's cousin Noorbaz Khan had finished his day's work at Afzal & Sons when he walked out of the Fort George army barracks with Omar, my cousin, to stretch his legs. They had cooked for the soldiers there, doing a brisk trade selling snacks, tea, coffee and cigarettes. They strolled carefree down Strand Road watching the sun set on the River Foyle as skylarks flew overhead.

This peace was shattered when a van pulled up alongside them, out of which two masked men jumped, pointing Browning pistols in their faces. Both Noorbaz and Omar were bundled into the back of the van, which drove a short distance before pulling over by the side of the road. It was the height of the Troubles, and these masked men were members of the Provisional IRA.

'I've got five children,' pleaded Noorbaz.

The two masked men levelled their weapons at him, then one of them spoke.

'You're a spy helping British intelligence. I don't care how many children you've got.'

He pulled the trigger, and Noorbaz's body hit the floor of the van. Then they turned to Omar.

'Get out.'

Omar stood in the road, the cold steel barrel of a gun still pressed against his temple.

'Now go and tell Mr Afzal to get out of Ireland,' they hissed. 'Or this will be his grave.'

It was Mum who, gently pulling me close, broke the news to me the next day. 'We're only on earth to pass the time,' she told me.

Noorbaz's body was returned to Birmingham soon afterwards for Janazah, the funeral prayers. At the mosque, I walked to the table where his open coffin lay. One of Noorbaz's sons was the same age as me and I shuddered at the thought of what he must be feeling. I could not imagine losing my own father in such a way. Noorbaz's body was covered in a white shroud, but his face was exposed and I stared at the bullet wound in his cheek. The wound was smaller than I thought it would be, and the rest of his face looked normal. Tranquil, even. I lingered by the coffin, lost in my thoughts.

As the prayers were recited, I mumbled along, not really knowing the words. Instead, I looked around me and watched everyone else, their heads bowed in deep reflection. I felt so many things: devastated at the loss, furious at the injustice of it all. And a little ashamed, too, that I hadn't known more about the conflict in Ireland and the dangers there. So I did the only thing I knew how to in these circumstances: I went to the library and got out every book I could find on the Troubles. I learned of so much that I hadn't been taught in schools. The tragic nature of the conflict, the losses on both sides. How the IRA were relentless in their pursuit of anyone deemed to be helping the security forces. But Noorbaz simply sold cigarettes and made tea for soldiers. Working all hours of the day, he rarely left the base. He most certainly wasn't a spy and it would be ridiculous to think otherwise.

I overheard my parents talking later that night.

'It's not safe,' Mum said. 'You have to leave.'

'That's what they want,' Dad replied. I could hear the grief in his voice, but there was defiance too, as he told her that he would honour Noorbaz's life by staying strong and refusing to capitulate.

'It could have been you that they killed,' she said, her voice gentler now.

'This is all I'm good at,' he said. 'This work pays for the roof over our heads, and the food on the table.' No one, not even a man with a gun, could change that.

I felt a new level of respect for Dad. I knew, of course, that he had worked in war zones during the Second World War. He had seen terrible things, some of the worst of humanity, and always seemed quite matter of fact about death. I knew he was risking his life for us and I knew that my brothers were in danger too, but I couldn't help admiring his bravery, his courage of conviction. I'd never properly understood the meaning of those words before. But I did now.

Later, I asked Dad if the men would ever be caught. He looked at me and shook his head. 'You don't get justice in this world, son. They'll get what they deserve in the afterlife.'

It was at that time that I began to take an interest in law as a career. Dad, though, was far from convinced that this was the best choice. After all, I didn't have the connections and at that time, they were key if you were to make it. My dad didn't know anyone working at the Bar. He couldn't turn to a friend at the golf club for help. I had no family member keeping a job warm for me. I was going to have to force my way into the club.

In 1983 I went to Birmingham University to study law and after I graduated, I applied to law school in Guildford. They had been training lawyers for over a hundred years and it was among the foremost places for Law Society training. I made my way down to Surrey for my interview, determined to get a place on the course. The tutor smiled curiously at me, before asking if I was sure this was what I wanted to do. It seemed it wasn't just Dad who wanted to discourage me. On my first day in class, I clocked immediately the fact that I was the only person there who wasn't white. My fellow students seemed as bewildered by me as I was by them.

I knew it wasn't going to be easy, and so it proved. I had an idealistic view of law and was excited to throw myself into the training, but over the next few years the lecturers did all they could to drum this out of me. What I'd hoped would be an enriching learning experience was, in fact, mind-numbing drudgery.

I got through my exams by learning lists. The list of documents to serve on a court in a family case, or in a probate case, or a company commercial litigation case; the documents you needed to set up a company, the documents you needed to serve on the court in a criminal litigation case, the documents you needed to obtain a divorce. Endless documents. It was list after list after list. The amount of independent thinking I had to do was minimal, the amount I learned about client care or victim care was minimal and the amount they taught you on empathy was, yes, minimal.

The whole process was thoroughly depressing, even soul-destroying. Mandela once said that 'education is the most powerful weapon which you can use to change the world'. But it was near impossible to equate my time in Guildford with such a lofty sentiment. I wasn't being prepared to change the world, I was just memorising lists. I was learning nothing to advance or develop me in the way I had hoped, and I became determined simply to get the qualification and get out of there.

I was starting to question whether my dad had been right after all. Was this really for me?

But just when I was losing hope, I finally found something I could get my teeth into. Criminal law. When I began to study it, it genuinely excited me, unlike nearly everything else I had come across in law. I knew immediately it was the path I wanted to take.

Criminal law was something I understood instinctively. Wherever you live, you tune in to how the community feels, how it perceives itself, and I knew I came from a frightened community. I had grown up in an area heavily affected by crime and seen how it affected the lives of those living there. I knew very well what it was like to walk out of your house in the morning and feel the comfort of family security dissolve into fear at the imminent threat of violence.

If you wanted to stay safe, you clung to family. There was no one to run to: the police at the bottom of the road treated you with disdain and we were as scared of them as we were of criminals. It was lonely. And it was dangerous. There is plenty of research showing that fear of crime is associated with poorer mental health, reduced confidence and lower quality of life. Fear holds communities back.

After finishing university, in the months before law school, I lived above my brother's shop for a while and would watch him try to make the building more secure, constantly adding lockable bolts and metal doors backed by reinforced steel rods – but still the burglars would find a way in and steal his takings. Crime was ubiquitous. It was intrinsic to the community's day-to-day existence, and to mine. Burglaries, violence, murder and anti-social behaviour, like being spat at and verbally abused, was part of life for me. There was an immediacy to criminal law, and I could feel the way it embodied my own experiences. It became very obvious to me that it was the only area I could and should work in.

After many months of struggling to concentrate in lectures because the subject matter was so dull, I was now on the edge of my seat, learning that there were consequences to criminal behaviour. Rights could be upheld and nobody was above the law – not even the police.

But while I was finally connecting with my studies, I was still painfully isolated in Guildford; I just couldn't find anyone to relate to on my course.

The only person I felt close to during my time there was an Irishwoman called Margaret, who was my landlady. On the surface, I didn't have much in common with her, a single Irish mother in her fifties with a room to spare. But like me, Margaret was an outsider.

In 1974, two pubs in Guildford were bombed by the IRA, killing four soldiers and one civilian, and wounding many more. A decade on and the scars were not yet healed. After years spent trying to hide her origins, Margaret now only had a soft burr of an Irish accent left. Anti-Irish prejudice was virulent, she explained, and it wasn't uncommon to be abused in the street if people heard an Irish accent. So naturally, she kept herself to herself.

Her house was a twenty-minute walk from the law school and it became a sanctuary for me, with its many shelves lined with books that I devoured. Often, I couldn't wait to get back there. By now, I had a part-time job in a local cinema foyer selling plastic caricatures from the TV programme *Spitting Image*. After a few hours selling Maggie Thatcher puppets in the evening (I didn't sell many Arthur Scargill ones there), I would buy some vegetables on the way home and bring them back to cook something for us both.

Margaret would come into the kitchen and put the kettle on, pulling up a chair as I cooked. She was fascinated by my repertoire of Pakistani recipes and watched with interest as I tried to make pakoras and dhal. There was no Asian grocer in Guildford so I had to make do with ingredients from Holland

& Barrett, which meant the results of my recipes were never quite as good as Mum's, whose cooking I desperately missed. I sensed kindness in Margaret, knowing that, at the time, many landlords weren't keen to take in someone with a brown face.

She was also curious. She wanted to know why my family had come to Britain, what their hopes were for their children. What, she asked, was the life they had left behind? I told her about the North West Frontier province in Pakistan, my dad's work for the British army and the better life they wanted for us.

'Sometimes you hear people say, "I was the first person in my family to go to university",' I said with a smile. 'We were the first generation to go to school. No one went to school in Pakistan. My dad started work at eight years old.'

Then I listened as Margaret told me what it was like to be an Irish immigrant in England. Although she had been here for many years now, she still felt like an outsider, particularly given the political tensions.

'I've just learned to hide it,' she said. 'I've taken my ex-husband's name and got rid of my accent. It's the only way to fit in.'

I poured another scoop of my pakora batter into the sizzling oil, thinking of the National Front goons I had become accustomed to seeing in Birmingham. Then she began to tell me how painful the IRA pub bombings were.

'They caused so much hurt, created so much hate. People still spit at me. I wonder when it's ever going to end.' But, she explained, there was so much pain in Ireland too. She would later teach me about Michael Collins, a leading figure in Ireland's struggle for independence, and we'd talk long into the night about the people who inspired us. I admired Gandhi, I told her, because he delivered the messages of the vulnerable to the people in authority.

The sizzling oil had cooled by now. I started to place the golden brown pakoras onto a sheet of kitchen roll. I knew about the IRA, I told her. They killed a member of my family.

Margaret's face went white.

'My God, I'm so sorry. What must you think of me?'

'Don't be daft,' I laughed. 'You weren't there. Come on, let's eat.'

By the end of the 1980s, I was finally practising law as a defence solicitor at the firm Glaisyers in Birmingham. After years of studying and thinking about the law, it was no longer abstract. I was dealing with real cases of rape, fraud and violent crime, and in my home city to boot. Some of these cases were significant. I hadn't been in the job very long when I found myself working on a major case against the West Midlands Serious Crime Squad, defending people who had been framed by a group of police officers. The case was being led by my supervisor, Ewen Smith, and he showed me how to overturn convictions and prove statements taken by the police had been falsified. He was extremely meticulous and taught me a life-long lesson of paying attention to detail.

These were the days before tape-recorded interviews, so police had to rely on handwritten records. It was also a time when you didn't have an automatic right to a solicitor when you were being interviewed by a police officer. According to the West Midlands Serious Crime Squad, lots of people in Birmingham had 'confessed' to a multitude of crimes. Those who had been charged begged to differ, arguing that they had been fitted up and their statements falsified by police. They may have been convicted of other crimes but they were adamant they had nothing to do with those crimes they were now being accused of by the police.

Ewen was able to prove that this falsification of statements had happened by using a specialised piece of equipment called an electrostatic detection device (EDD), which could look at the imprints on witness statements and show what had been added or taken away. The EDD worked by stretching a Mylar film (like clingfilm, essentially) over a document, which was then electrostatically charged to create an electronic image of indentations from the lower sheet. When these were compared to the higher sheet, it was possible to see whether the document had been changed in some way since its original composition. Using this technology, we were able to prove that statements had been tampered with, usually by the addition of incriminating phrases. In the case of one of our clients, a single line admission to the offence had even been added to his statement by interviewing detectives.

As a result, the West Midlands Serious Crime Squad was in due course shut down. At least forty convictions made in the 1980s were, it was proved, the result of malpractice. They were subsequently overturned. It was a phenomenal success for us, and a galvanising first case to work on. Victims were acquitted by the Court of Appeal while police officers were prosecuted for perjury and perverting the course of justice.

This was criminal law happening for real, not confined to a textbook. What had ignited my interest in lecture theatres a year earlier was now happening right in front of me. My teachers had been correct all along: nobody was above the law.

So it should have been my dream job. And yes, it had been exhilarating to work with Ewen and pull our case together: identifying when officers were in the police station, who else was in the interview room and whether they could have been on duty at the time the statements had been taken. It felt groundbreaking. And yet – something just wasn't quite right. I was about to find out what that was.

The skill of a defence lawyer is the ability to discredit the case made against a client. They spend their time looking for holes and inconsistencies. These are like threads – tug at enough of them and the entire case soon unravels. But I would often find myself reading through case reports and admiring the handiwork of my opposite number, appreciating the skill that had been necessary to *build* the case. I was beginning to realise that I was more interested in making a case than tearing one apart.

Things came to a head in a custody suite in 1990, when I was taking instruction from a client who had been accused of rape. The cardinal rule of our profession is that a lawyer cannot make false representation to the court. In other words, if a client confesses his guilt to their lawyer, then they must cease representing them – although I'm sure some lawyers say to their clients, 'Don't tell me you did it, otherwise I can't represent you if you want to plead not guilty.' This principle established a lawyer's duty to the court.

That day, I took my seat and began as I always did, by asking the man if he committed the offence of which he had been accused.

'Did you rape this woman?'

He leaned back in his chair and put his arms behind his head. Before he had even opened his mouth, he seemed to be laughing at me, a vulpine grin creeping across his face.

'Nah, course I didn't. That's why you're here.'

I took a sip of water and shuffled my papers. I had read the case file closely, and knew there was powerful evidence against this man. In this instance, from the evidence in front of me, I suspected he was guilty. I presented him with the woman's statement.

I watched him take a cruel pleasure in reading through the details of her ordeal. The suspect took his time, as though he was recalling the events and savouring every moment. He had known the woman in question; had been stalking her for over six months. He had regularly turned up at her workplace and pestered her, and she had reported him to the police numerous times. There was plenty of evidence documenting this. Then he started appearing outside her home and, one night, when he knew she was alone, he forced his way in and raped the victim.

'But what about the damage to the door?' I asked him, studying the case file.

'It was already damaged. That was nothing to do with me. The sex was . . . Consensual. Yeah, that's the word.'

He was lying. I knew it, felt it. I rummaged through my papers, pretending to be looking for an important detail that would help his case so I could have a moment to think. My job was to defend this man, and I was going to have to make a bail application to put him back on the street. But I didn't believe in this work and I didn't believe in him. I couldn't do this. All I wanted to do was reach across the desk and throttle him.

But it was my job. I had to do it and I did, advising him to say 'no comment' under questioning. I made the bail application, and it was successful. The next day the man was back out on the street, although of course with strict conditions not to approach the victim. However, he was still free to harm others – or even to go back to her, if he was really determined to do so. To me, this was not acceptable.

His face had told me he was going to enjoy putting his victim through the wringer in court. She was going to have to relive everything all over again and might even be accused of lying. Maybe he would even get off.

I couldn't play any further part in helping him.

That same day, I went back to my office and handed in my resignation.

I was conflicted. Of course, I absolutely believed in the right to a fair trial. It is an essential safeguard of a just society. Every person accused of a crime should have their guilt or innocence determined by a rigorous legal process. That's the rule of law, and couldn't work without defence solicitors. They are essential. But I couldn't play that role anymore.

I knew other people who had come to the same conclusion. Indeed, some of my colleagues had left the legal profession altogether after successfully defending people who they suspected were guilty of heinous crimes – and it was subsequently proved that they were.

There was another reason I gave in my notice that day. Working in a general practice meant I was also doing probate, wills and trust work, together with some commercial law. And I was bored. Yet even though I had little interest in it, I was reasonably good at these lines of work and as a result, I had started to fear I would soon be expected to specialise in them. I had by now spent months worrying about this possibility. That afternoon, with that client, had given me the push I needed.

By the time Christmas 1990 came around, I was unemployed with little in the way of prospects for the New Year. My parents were understandably worried, not least because they knew other things were going wrong in my life: my marriage had broken down.

I had met Penny, an Irish Catholic, at Birmingham University, towards the end of my time there. Finally, I had found someone to whom I could relate. We hurriedly married in 1987 at the University Chaplaincy. Penny's mother was a divorcee living in Scarborough and she reluctantly accepted me, even though she kept referring to my 'olive skin', which confused me no end – I had only ever seen green olives.

It caused problems with my own family immediately, however, as they detested the idea of me being in a relationship with a white, non-Muslim woman. (I couldn't help but think their views were odd, given my uncle's marriage to a white woman. It seemed that as the first generation born in the UK, we couldn't be allowed such choices.)

When my brothers first asked me to stop seeing Penny, I was sitting with them in the lounge at home. When I started to say 'I love her', one of them slapped me hard across the face before the words had even left my mouth.

For a couple of years it was a happy marriage, while I qualified as a solicitor and she worked as a BBC production trainee. I was pulling long hours, however, and we started to grow apart. Consumed by my job, I didn't realise she was unhappy. Unbeknown to me, she started an affair with a fellow BBC producer.

The first I knew of it was when I came home from work in

November 1990 and found half our stuff missing. I thought the house had been burgled. Then I noticed a Post-it note on the table. It read: 'Don't be sad. I have left you for Martin. I will be in touch.'

Of course I was sad, I was devastated. How could I not be? Angry, too, and at times guilty, ashamed – not to mention lonely. However, I drew strength from the support of my family, especially as they never once said, 'I told you so.' They knew how troubled I was at work and how keen I was to find a job where I could grow, where I could be happy.

No matter how bruising my experience in the world of defence had proved, it hadn't changed how I felt about the law more broadly. I wanted to stay in the field and was becoming interested in prosecution, which only fairly recently had undergone enormous, and long overdue, structural change.

The Crown Prosecution Service was established in 1986 to make prosecuting decisions independent of the police, who until then had been responsible for prosecuting all cases. In 1962, a Royal Commission reported that it was 'undesirable' for police officers to also appear as prosecutors, given the potential conflicts of interest. While this brought some change to the haphazard and rather amateurish manner in which prosecutions were conducted, with some police forces creating prosecuting solicitors' departments to handle this aspect of proceedings, the changes didn't go far enough to address the problems at the heart of public prosecutions. Disquiet continued to grow, particularly when convictions obtained unfairly in the 1970s were subsequently overturned by the Court of Appeal.

One of these cases was the tipping point for the second Royal Commission. In 1972, police jailed three teenagers for the murder of Maxwell Confait after forcing confessions from them under pressure, following interviews conducted without access to a lawyer, parent or guardian. This was in breach of police guidelines at the time, for they were all underage. One of them even had learning difficulties.

All the convictions were ultimately overturned as the confessions had been obtained unfairly. The police were widely criticised, viewed as a law unto themselves. Change could no longer be resisted – but the wheels of government grind slowly, and it took until 1981 for a second Royal Commission to lay bare the unfairness, inefficiency and lack of accountability that were then at the heart of the criminal justice system. The Commission concluded that the police could no longer retain the responsibility for prosecutions except for the most minor crimes, such as traffic or regulatory offences.

The Commission argued that a Crown Prosecution Service had to be created that would be separate from the police in the interests of fairness, to 'make the conduct of prosecution the responsibility of someone who is both legally qualified and is not identified with the investigative process'. Therefore, in 1983 a White Paper proposed an independent prosecution service for England and Wales. This led to the

Prosecution of Offences Act, and the Crown Prosecution Service was born in 1986.

For my generation, who had grown up learning about such gross miscarriages of justice as the Guildford Four and Maguire Seven, the Birmingham Six and the Bridgewater Four among others, this was an entirely necessary, and long overdue, development.

Naturally, the change met with considerable resistance from the police, chiefly because it represented a significant reduction in their power. But it was a vital change for the integrity of sentencing. Although I could see how much prosecutors were struggling with their limited resources in this fledgling operation, I immediately felt a calling: it was an area where I could develop my skills, and it would also be exciting to be on the front line of these changes. At the very least, it would provide a break from the strict hierarchy of law firms.

After Christmas I wrote to the Chief Crown Prosecutor in London, Brian McArdle, offering my services. It was a long shot but I prayed it would come off. By now, I was desperate to get out of Birmingham.

It wasn't just the breakdown of my relationship and the end of my job making my home city feel claustrophobic. Birmingham was a different place now. The city of my youth in the 1960s and 1970s felt like a place of drive and ambition. Even though I often came home covered in spit because racist skinheads hung around street corners harassing ethnic minorities, there was still a sense that people were achieving. Everyone we knew worked, many of them seven days a week. We were busy making things happen and our community was strong.

However, now political changes saw a sustained period of deindustrialisation. Nearly one in four of all manufacturing jobs had disappeared in Margaret Thatcher's first term and the West Midlands was hit hard. Unemployment rocketed in the 1980s – reaching 10.8 per cent in 1982, the highest since the Great Depression – and industrial decline started to set in across the city. Communities were devastated and Birmingham no longer seemed the dynamic city it had once been for me.

Local reggae band UB40 summed up the mood of the time with their song 'One in Ten', in which Ali Campbell sang of how it felt to be 'a statistic, a reminder of a world that doesn't care'. The spectral moan of the synthesiser, and the blaring brass of the Specials' 'Ghost Town' was the soundtrack to the sense of social breakdown all around me. I wanted to go to London now, because there were more opportunities there for me to progress. My mum understood. The way she saw it, I was following my father's dream, because he had loved London when he first arrived in England but had been obliged to move to Birmingham to support his family. I had no such ties.

In March 1991, I received a letter from the Crown Prosecution Service inviting me for an interview for a temporary contract to join the Westminster branch. I packed my bags and headed to Birmingham New Street Station to get the next train to London. I could feel the weight of months of sorrow lifting from me at last. I wasn't going to fail. I paced the platform waiting for my train and stared down the tracks to London, where I knew my future lay. I was going to be a prosecutor.

III

The place was absolutely jumping. And the music was loud. Really loud. I could feel the Bhangramuffin fusion coursing through my chest. Under the strobing lights and lasers, a sea of people was bobbing up and down to the high-energy, trance-inducing beat of Apache Indian's 'Chok There'.

Looking down on the dance floor, I took hold of the mic and began working the crowd, shouting God knows what until a riotous climax of energy washed over me. It felt like an unstoppable force was carrying me. I may have been only 125 miles away from Birmingham, but Camden in the early 1990s was light years away from the life I had left behind.

Just as I was arriving in the city, a new cultural energy was sweeping through London and it was felt most keenly in places like Camden. There was a freshness and a freedom that was utterly new to me. Musically, too, it was a place where cultures blended and collided: a melting pot of jungle, rave, house, garage, Britpop and drum 'n' bass. It was music I'd listened to at home, but now I could actually experience it. I became a frequent visitor to HQs at Camden Lock and got talking to Keith, the man mountain who worked the door. He told me his dream was to put on his own club night. And I told him we should do it.

Keith introduced me to Thanos, the club's Greek owner, who didn't seem too interested in us at first. He was far too busy complaining that his coffee machine was always broken. So, doing what I knew best, I wrote a letter to the supplier and got it properly, permanently fixed. Suddenly, Thanos couldn't do enough for me. Within weeks, we had arranged a Wednesday residency. It wasn't long before we were bringing in big name DJs: Paul 'Trouble' Anderson, Funkmaster Flex and Jazzie B from Soul II Soul, they all did sets for us. It was surreal, but I loved it.

Each Wednesday we would finish at 2am, check the takings and I'd be on my way, home for 3am to catch a few hours of sleep before walking to my day job as a prosecutor in Victoria. The Crown Prosecution Service was based on the twenty-third floor of Portland House.

The sense of freedom I felt in those early days in London was incredibly empowering. The sheer diversity was intoxicating. Every day, I was meeting people from all over the world. Muslims in London come from over fifty countries, while in Birmingham they hail mainly from two. For the first time in my life, being different was something to celebrate, and I stopped fearing a racist attack whenever I left the house. I'd spent a large part of my childhood dodging threats, not to mention spit, on the very streets that had seen Enoch Powell making his famous 'Rivers of Blood' speech. Now I was free. And even better than that, I loved my job.

As a prosecutor I was at the vanguard of change. We were bringing rigour to an area that had escaped its jurisdiction for too long. But in order to understand the challenge we faced, how prosecution works has to be understood.

The job of a prosecutor is to bring criminals to justice, and two 'tests' must be cleared before a decision to prosecute is made. The first one is the evidential test: you have to be satisfied that, based on the evidence you have before you, there is a realistic prospect of conviction. This means you must believe that it's more likely than not that the person in question will be proved guilty. If you cross this threshold, then there is the second test to apply – the public interest test. Is it in the public interest to charge this person?

A prosecution will usually take place unless there are public interest factors that outweigh those in favour of prosecution. The more serious the crime, the more likely that it will be in the public interest. In the case of homicide, rape and robbery, for example, there is no doubt in my mind that those cases should be prosecuted, and that the public would expect and indeed require it. But there are some instances in which it would not necessarily be in the public interest to prosecute a case. For example, I once dealt with a medical student who was in her final year at university, on course to become fully qualified as a doctor. She had gone out on the town with her friends and, having drunk too much, thought it would be a good idea to remove the tyres from a vehicle and put it on bricks. The vehicle fell off those bricks and caused a sizeable amount of criminal damage. She was subsequently arrested and admitted to the crime. This offence clearly passed the evidential test, but in weighing up the public interest I could see that the young student didn't go out with a view to causing damage. It was a one-off situation, she was remorseful and were she to get a conviction for this, she probably wouldn't be able to qualify as a doctor. Considering these factors, I decided that the greater need was for her to finish her studies to become a doctor. Therefore, there was no public interest in prosecuting her. Giving her a conviction would have been detrimental to both the girl and to society, deprived of her service as a doctor. So instead, she was only ordered to pay compensation for the damage.

The public interest test is problematic because while there is guidance on how it should be applied, ultimately it relies on a judgment call from prosecutors. However, our evidential tests did improve the quality of the cases that made it to court. Before the creation of the CPS, the evidential test was much more nebulous, far less rigorous. 'Let's give it a punt' used to be the police catch-cry to start a prosecution, closely followed by, 'let's see what the jury thinks'. This created the perfect environment for miscarriages of justice based on insufficient, or inappropriate, evidence. With an independent prosecution service, that ended.

While bringing a more professional approach to prosecution was something we were all trying to achieve and could take satisfaction from, there were many more challenging aspects to the job that no one told you about at interview.

I had been warned by former colleagues at Glaisyers that the CPS was poorly resourced, and told it would be a backwards career step, but I was so anxious to be free that I didn't take much notice of this until I started the job.

There was one challenge I hadn't foreseen: virtually everyone we worked with hated us. The police didn't like us because of the loss of power we had caused and continued to represent, while the magistrates hated us because they were used to working with police barristers and we did things differently. Early on in my career, I had to tell a magistrate the prosecution had decided there was insufficient evidence to continue a case. The magistrate refused to accept the discontinuation and began arguing with me.

'You can't do this, he's been charged,' he began.

'Sir, the 1985 Prosecution of Offences Act gives me the power to do so, and I'm doing it,' I told him.

'No, you can't!' he said, raising his voice. 'I'll put this case back so you can come back in later and we can carry on.'

'No! We're not carrying on. I am dropping this case. It is

my statutory right to do so. I've made a judgment that there is insufficient evidence.'

'No, I've put this case back to the end of the list so you can come back in and reconsider your decision.'

'Sir, you cannot stop me!'

The exchange went on and on like this. It was an environment where change was anathema. They weren't used to our approach and the police hardly ever dropped a case. Every day was a battle with the magistrates. By now, we were five years into the CPS and there remained a determined refusal from some quarters to accept our independence. But we didn't take a punt. We did our job.

Although it was exhilarating and no day was the same, it was therefore also quite a lonely job at times – not to mention exhausting, as we were worked off our feet with nothing like the preparation time solicitors had. Despite the attritional nature of the job, though, I relished every day. It was exciting and you didn't know what to expect. This was what I wanted to do.

My enthusiasm for the work didn't go unnoticed and soon I was being handed tricky cases. The CPS had extremely limited resources at that time, and so if you wanted to do well, you had to make things happen yourself. In the early days, the CPS struggled to recruit and had fewer than 3,500 staff, of whom 1,250 were lawyers. In under a decade, this increased to 6,000 staff, including 2,000 lawyers. Between 2000 and 2005 the government doubled the CPS budget, but in the early

1990s we had to make do and operate on a shoestring. And this meant we were often failing to keep up.

When I joined the CPS, it was suggested that only one crime in fifty was leading to a conviction, yet at the same time crime rates were soaring in the 1990s – Lord Birt would later estimate that 130 million serious offences may have been committed in a single year. Public confidence in justice was low and British Crime Surveys in the late 1990s showed that, of all the criminal justice agencies, the CPS scored lower than the police, prisons and probation service in terms of the percentage of people (25 per cent) who felt they were doing a good job; only judges scored worse. Our job was to change both that perception and the number of cases being prosecuted, but it was not going to be easy.

When I first started work in London, I was sent to the court at Horseferry Road. It was the busiest in the country, and was also where the Chief Magistrate of England and Wales sat. I began working on road traffic trials, which was something of a challenge – I didn't drive, so had some catching up to do on the laws of the road, devouring the Highway Code at my desk. I often prosecuted half a dozen of these cases a day, learning as I worked and gaining vital trial experience. On a few occasions I prosecuted some celebrities too, which would pit me against their very experienced – and expensive – team of lawyers. Winning these cases felt great, and gave me the confidence to seek out tougher challenges.

The only thing that tempered my enthusiasm for the job was the hard-drinking culture. As a teetotaller, I was never comfortable with the pressure to be at the pub constantly but it felt like, if you wanted to get ahead, there was simply no way of avoiding it. Early on I was told I *had* to come along to these gatherings. It simply wouldn't look good if I opted out. *You must come to the pub if you want to get on here, Nazir. This is how it works. You want to know about opportunities, don't you?* I headed, somewhat reluctantly, to Ye Olde Cheshire Cheese on Fleet Street, where every solicitor and barrister seemed to gather of an evening. So, I thought: this is what the old boys' club looks like.

It was quite the contrast to my nights in Camden. I sat awkwardly at the bar, nursing a Coke while trying to suppress a growing nausea. The gin vapours that hung in the air and the sharp, sour smell of lager didn't help. Neither did the braying laughter that permeated every discussion. The only opportunity that ever came my way here was the chance to see people get incredibly drunk – and talk about themselves and any judge they didn't like.

No one ever spoke about the people we were supposed to be helping and if you tried to talk seriously about work, you were likely to be mocked. So much for working for others.

C'mon Nazir, lighten up and raise your glass. A toast, everyone. In the interests of just us! Every week, that laughter followed me out of the door and stayed with me as I made my way home.

On these evenings, I started to doubt the work I was doing, or at least the place I was doing it. I knew from my own experience that large swathes of Britain had no faith in the justice system. As a child I had seen crime everywhere, had experienced it myself and knew that my people, at home on the streets of Birmingham, felt that the legal system was for others. People with money and social status. Certainly my early experiences of legal culture didn't do much to change my mind.

It was ironic, then, that as much as I loathed the drinking habits that seemed to bind everyone else, my sobriety would eventually give me the opportunity to get ahead and climb the ranks.

A key figure at the CPS at the time was Jeff McCann, a special casework lawyer who did most of the serious high-profile cases. Jeff was an outstanding lawyer but I soon had reason to suspect that he struggled with his drinking, so much so that he would sometimes find it difficult to function in the afternoon. Coming back from the morning court together, I would offer to help him with his cases, and he would be happy to accept.

Despite this, I learned a huge amount from Jeff. He was old school and knew much more about law than me. Like Ewen Smith, he understood the importance of detail and was assiduous in preparing cases. He had spent many years as a defence lawyer so could see both sides of a case. He would usually know what the defence strategy would be, so would start plugging gaps before our opponents could make their arguments. Because he was so networked, he would look at cases and tell us straight away the level of resource we needed based on who was on the other side. 'This firm are good,' he would warn us. 'You all need to do your job and up your game.' On other occasions, such as once when I was gathering continuity evidence in a drugs case to demonstrate that the drugs in court were the same items seized during an investigation, he would tell me not to bother. 'I know who is on the other side, Nazir. They're not very good and they're not going to be interested in continuity. Don't worry.'

He also had a big personality and didn't take things too seriously. Jeff was always laughing and bringing levity to proceedings. It was probably a coping mechanism, but when you're dealing with murder cases and looking at pictures of deceased people it is not something you should be able to find humour in, but Jeff would. As a result, I would go home thinking about Jeff's bad jokes, rather than having the images of victims in my mind. His was a strangely reassuring presence, and it helped me get through some tough days.

Jeff was also empathetic and, like me, wanted the CPS to be a people-focused organisation. Early on, he said something that I would repeat religiously to my team years later. 'Every statement is a person,' he said. 'Don't ever forget that.' He told us that it was easy to turn over the page and forget that there was a person behind the words on the page. It was his way of telling us not to go into a courtroom clutching a file thinking, *I just have to process this case*. You would always make better decisions if you thought of the impact of crime, and the people behind the statements.

Jeff was brave, too, and even on his last day working for the CPS in 1996 he was still in the thick of it, holding his own on the front line. On that particular occasion, things went far beyond verbal jousting and he ended up being physically attacked in court by Matthew Simmons, the Crystal Palace football fan who attained notoriety after the Manchester United footballer, Eric Cantona, kung fu-kicked him. Simmons had been found guilty of using threatening words and behaviour during the incident and, as Jeff started to apply for an order to exclude him from football grounds, Simmons leapt over a bench and attacked him, kicking Jeff in the chest, grabbing his collar and swinging at him before police dragged him away. Simmons was jailed for seven days for contempt of court. Jeff dusted himself down and politely declined to press charges.

My work with Jeff had given me exposure to different, more serious cases and as a result I was able to do more demanding work. Now I was in a courtroom five days a week, often working to challenging deadlines. Working the remand court, where people who have been held in custody make their first court appearance, was a case in point: I was often given several new cases in the morning to deal with that same day, and had to learn to speed read, think on my feet and find the salient facts. The remand court decided whether these people were to be released on bail and set trial dates for criminal cases.

I only saw case files for the first time a short period, sometimes a few minutes, before I went to court, so had to absorb everything quickly, particularly as I could have as many as eighty or ninety cases to deal with every day that related to people who had been arrested overnight – and some of these were serious. They could include rapes and homicide, or drugs and fraud cases, often with complex details. I would aim to get through as many of them as possible and hope that some of the other courts would finish early so there might be a chance for them to take the remaining cases off my hands. It was often chaotic. But while I certainly wouldn't recommend it now, in many ways it was the making of me.

Locking horns with the tough district judges that presided over these cases provided another important part of my learning. Rosamond Keating, Roger Davis and Geoffrey Breen took no prisoners and they would go for the jugular if they spotted a lawyer winging it when a case was slipping away from them, which inevitably happened occasionally when a lawyer was handling dozens of cases a day. Once, I incurred the wrath of a judge when I tried to make an application to remand the suspect of a relatively minor offence in custody on the grounds he would re-offend. He was as quick as anything, and I was scrabbling to catch up with the facts in my case file.

'What's your evidence?' he asked sharply.

'Sir, it's a very serious offence,' I replied, trying to sound convincing.

'You may think it's a serious offence, but of course we haven't proven that yet, have we? He's innocent until proven guilty is he not?'

'He may well be sir,' I replied, 'but, err, the evidence is very strong.'

His brow furrowed. 'Do you have the evidence, then?'

'I have a statement from the victim,' I countered.

'Do you have any evidence that links the defendant with this crime?'

'I will have, sir. If you give me a week.'

He shook his head and smiled.

'You don't know what you're talking about, do you?'

It was relentless – and often dysfunctional. I could see from the beginning that even the best lawyers would struggle to do their job consistently in this kind of environment. Before Davis in Court One once, I was working through a trial list, which is a number of short trials listed one after the other, when Davis beckoned me over.

'Mrs Keating has a trial involving a police officer in Court Three, and no one's turned up to prosecute. Can you do it?'

'But I'm here with you,' I said, confused.

'Yes, I know. Can you go and start her trial and then come back to mine? You can return to cross examine her defendant when this trial's finished.'

I stammered an agreement.

'Well, you'd better get going, then,' he said.

So off I ran to Court Three and started one trial, then ran back to Court One where I started another, calling the trials officer forth to give his evidence. Then I returned to Court Three and called the officer there to give his evidence, before returning to Court One, by which time the defendant was in the stand, waiting to be cross-examined. And then I went back to Court Three to do the same again, before returning to Court One to hear Davis convict the defendant and sentence him. At this point, I was almost dizzy, but I prosecuted both cases successfully, achieving convictions in two different courtrooms before two different judges. That's what summary justice was like in the 1990s.

It was only when key performance indicators were introduced that we started the process of dragging the system into the twenty-first century. Nowadays, everything is measured from how long a case takes to prepare, how long a case lasts, the reasons for certain case outcomes, compliance with national prosecution policies, average number of hearings per case. This would allow us to measure our successes, and our failures, in much more detail.

Before that, however, justice was a messy, make-it-up-as-you-go madhouse that would have sent most sane people rushing to the job centre to change career. We were allowed to make mistakes then, because when you had thousands of cases going through the courts, you simply didn't have the opportunity to dot all the i's and cross all the t's. You had to make quick judgments, whereas decision-making takes a lot longer in the more modern, regulated system, meaning that, each case is also under more scrutiny, particularly in the world of social media.

Those higher up at the CPS had started to notice me – and so had the police. The relationship between the two continued to be strained, mainly because we didn't understand each other and what we were both trying to do. The police felt, wrongly in my view, that we were too victim-oriented, focusing wholly on protecting the innocent, and weren't really on their side, the side of securing a conviction. It was true that we had this background, driven by a need to protect, but it was perfectly possible to both protect the innocent and convict the guilty. That was, in fact, the name of the game.

Many officers also didn't understand the specific level of evidence we needed to make a case. They continued to operate at a much lower evidence threshold to us, as they had done when they handled prosecutions directly, and after they had made an arrest they were frequently annoyed to find out that we felt differently. We had to prove a case beyond a reasonable doubt; the police could just arrest someone on reasonable suspicion. Our culture was 'show me the evidence'; their culture was 'we know he's guilty'. But this often meant that a defence would be able to rip their cases apart.

To prove a case, you need to have each element of the offence as specified in the law. For example, the theft act requires the 'dishonest' 'appropriation' of 'property' 'belonging to another': you need to prove that somebody took something dishonestly that amounted to property in law and belonged to another person. A house, for example, is counter-intuitively not property in that sense. It's a civil matter, not a criminal matter. The question of belonging can be challenging if there's a dispute over ownership.

But neither did we prosecutors fully understand the work the police were doing. We operated in a vacuum and didn't engage with the public at all, whereas the police operated on a 'policing by consent' model, meaning that to achieve success, they needed public approval, the faith of the public. This guiding philosophy has been described by the police historian Charles Reith as 'unique in history and throughout the world because it derived not from fear but public co-operation with the police'. But it only works when all communities feel their voices are being heard, and the public believes that the police are at their service.

The 1985 Prosecution of Offences Act, which created the CPS, stated that prosecutors must be independent. The traditional interpretation of this was that we had to be detached; we couldn't talk to the public because if we did it would somehow impact on our impartial decision-making. This also meant we kept our distance from the police – but I was starting to think that, if we could have more honest conversations, we might all be more successful at our jobs.

It frustrated me that we seemed to be worlds apart, because I could see that really, we were working to the same common goal of delivering justice. I started to make an effort to talk meaningfully with the police. I was fed up of trying to get shaky cases over the line, knowing their evidence was unlikely to make it through the rigorous process of the court. I needed them to understand what I needed. Whenever I got the opportunity I would visit a Detective Inspector at CID and ask them why they thought their case was going to succeed.

'Don't worry, Nazir. He's a wrong 'un,' was often the reply. 'Just get him in front of a jury.' I would suggest mildly that it was unlikely that the defendant would make it in front of the jury, because according to what I could see, the evidence simply wasn't there. They might have some good intelligence or a few connections, but often not quite enough to make the case work. Compelling though those leads could be, they wouldn't necessarily stand up in court. Intelligence wasn't evidence.

In these cases, I would often make a radical suggestion: drop the case now and use the intelligence to build a stronger case. Go out and gather more evidence, carry out more surveillance, do whatever was necessary to strengthen the case.

The DIs weighed up my words, often with a scratch of the head. But they could see my logic and more and more often, we would agree that this was the best course of action. Slowly, the distance between us was becoming surmountable and we were beginning to work together more effectively.

My office was half a mile away from New Scotland Yard and I started to find myself dropping in on the way to court to meet with senior officers. This was considered inappropriate by some of my colleagues, who thought the police should always come to us for a conference meeting where minutes were taken. We had to make it clear that we were in charge.

But anyone who sat in those meetings could see the dynamic wasn't working. It was just hierarchical posturing. Informal chats over a cup of tea in the canteen were far more productive. That's where officers would bounce ideas around, run cases by me and ask for my view so I could help them at an early investigative stage.

That's how I found myself involved in the case to catch the London serial killer who came to be known as the 'gay slayer'.

Colin Ireland was thirty-eight years old and an unemployed former soldier when he decided to begin murdering gay men in March 1993. He would pick up his victims at the Coleherne pub in Earl's Court before going back to their homes where he would torture and kill them.

After killing his first victim, a theatre director, Ireland called the Samaritans to tell them he had left two dogs locked up at the home of the person he had murdered, and someone needed to come and free them. He also called the *Sun* newspaper to tell them about the murder, adding that he wanted to be famous for being a serial killer. When the media reported that Ireland was an 'animal lover' he killed the cat of another victim and called the *Sun* again to tell them about it. 'Pet lover, am I?' he sneered.

Immediately we knew we were on to someone who was both terrifying and extremely challenging to bring to justice. Ireland was meticulous in disposing of evidence, and simultaneously the police were struggling to build a relationship with

London's gay community in order to source information about the crimes and the victims. Ireland sought men who were into sadomasochistic sex, and because sadomasochistic sex between consenting adults had recently been made illegal, people were understandably concerned that by co-operating they could be prosecuted for their private passions.

Three other killings swiftly followed, and the gay community became increasingly unsettled. Ireland called Kensington police to claim responsibility for all four murders, warning that he had to be stopped. But he was also starting to make mistakes. At the flat of a victim in Dalston, Ireland forgot to wipe his fingerprints off a metal bar that ran across the window. Finally, we had something – the smallest bit of evidence. However, we only had half a fingerprint for Ireland, and I knew it would not be admissible in court.

'It's not enough,' I said to officers. 'We need sixteen points for a match in a court of law.'

We had to redouble our efforts. Gay police officers were drafted in to build better relationships with the community, surveillance was increased and Detective Chief Superintendent Ken John went on television to appeal directly to Ireland. 'Speak to me,' he said. 'I want to speak to you. I need to speak to you. Enough is enough. Enough pain, enough anxiety, enough tragedy.'

But Ireland continued to kill. Another victim, a Maltese chef, was strangled to death in Catford. This time, however, we finally got a break.

Ireland had travelled to Catford with his victim, Emanuel Spiteri, on a Saturday night and footage from a British Rail CCTV security camera captured them both. The footage was blurred but it was something that police could put on a wanted poster and use to appeal for help in identifying him. Ireland saw the poster and went to see his solicitor, saying he was the man caught on the CCTV footage. But he wasn't the killer, he claimed, as he'd left Spiteri with another man because he didn't want a threesome. The police came straight to his flat at Southend and arrested him.

With the CCTV footage and the fingerprint, he was charged with two murders – but I knew we didn't have enough evidence to convict him. Ireland wasn't saying anything, and half a fingerprint and some blurry CCTV footage weren't going to cut it in the courtroom. We couldn't prosecute yet.

The police were frantically searching for more evidence when I met with a criminologist, Professor David Wilson, to see if we could get any other insights. Wilson told me that the killer was a narcissist, that he was proud of his crimes and that, if we could keep him long enough, he may confess to them.

I sensed he was probably right and our best hope of getting a conviction rested on Ireland himself. How long, though, would it take before he decided to talk? We were now coming under serious pressure from the defence team, who were demanding that we release him if we didn't have enough evidence. The magistrate was of the same view. We continued to ask for a few more weeks while we carried out further inquiries. We were stretching the period for preparation of the case for committal as long as we possibly could, in the hope and expectation that Ireland would give us everything we wanted.

This time, I communicated closely with the police. While I went to court, pleading with the magistrate to give us another week, the police carried out further inquiries in relation to the second murder. Because Ireland had spent time in Germany, officers travelled overseas to see if we could glean any new information this way. We were buying ourselves time and the magistrate sensed it: neither he nor the defence team were in the best of moods. Worse, our inquiries in Germany provided nothing new. We were running out of road.

I changed tack. I tried to convince the magistrate that we needed more time to look at potential witnesses in relation to the *fourth* murder. I kept coming up with anything to give us another week. But the magistrate's patience was running out. In a matter of days, when the next hearing date arrived, we knew he was going to release Ireland on bail. We were about to lose him. And I was certain he would kill again.

I had almost conceded defeat and was already thinking of what bail conditions would be appropriate for his release when, out of the blue, I got a phone call from the prison.

'Ireland has asked to be re-interviewed.'

I could feel my heart beating with joy as I hung up. Finally, we had our breakthrough. I knew it. We had found a way to keep him on the ropes. And now Ireland was going to confess.

And confess he did. He told the police everything. How he did it, why he did it and how others had escaped his grasp. He divulged every last graphic, gruesome detail and admitted that he would have carried on killing if he had not been caught. Suddenly, we had everything we needed. Ireland was sentenced to life and indeed died in prison in 2012.

The police came in for a fair bit of criticism over the Ireland case, particularly with their handling of the sexual orientation of the crimes. There were lessons to be learned. But I felt there were also some positive outcomes: the CPS had worked with the police effectively, and we'd got the result we all wanted. We had remedied the suspicions between both parties and if we could collaborate even earlier, I knew we could have even greater successes.

By now, I was regularly meeting with senior detectives in the Organised Crime Unit. The scale of the national crime problem was becoming clear: the enormity of the crime under investigation in the UK was huge. My job was to help them find ways to prioritise. I might look at cases where the police had nineteen serious criminal gangs under surveillance, for example, and I'd examine which cases were closest to being able to be brought to court. I could easily see which cases would take a week to get the necessary evidence, as well as those which might take up to three months and others six months to meet the evidence threshold. As resources were so stretched, we concentrated on efficiency, focusing on the cases that could be delivered quickly.

It was a steep learning curve, and I was now encountering offences of the utmost severity. I was invited by DCI Bob McLachlan, then head of the Paedophile Unit of Scotland Yard, to begin sharing details of investigations with a view to securing prosecutions. This was something new for them: they hadn't been this open with the CPS before, not formally, and I keenly felt the responsibility of getting it right.

The detectives there talked me through the very early stages of child abuse cases and suspects they had identified, asking for advice on the evidence they needed to bring them in successfully. To do that, they had to show me things that not only turned my stomach but changed me forever. When you see an eighteen-month-old child sexually abused on video, the world no longer seems the same.

This was a different level of depravity, and, as I looked around the room at the detectives I was getting to know, I was struck by the intensity of their work. DCI McLachlan, DS Andy Ryden and DI Ian Hughes were a breed apart, and had helped put some absolute monsters behind bars, including people who had tried to procure babies for sex. They were incredibly committed detectives, spending up to twelve hours a day looking at images of children being abused, studying video footage and images in painstaking detail in order to seek clues about perpetrators and evidence to bring about arrests. Then they had to go back home to their families and try and switch off. I couldn't imagine doing that kind of work. DS Ryden later confided in me that, when his first child was born and he held his daughter in his arms for the first time, he was overwhelmed by the thought that there were people in the world who were abusing children of that age.

Working with this team, it was not possible for me to say there was no case to answer, as I often did when evidence didn't meet the threshold for prosecution. I changed my way of thinking: what I needed to say instead was 'Yes, there could be a case to answer – if we take a different approach.' The difficulty was irrelevant: here, I focused on solutions, like briefing undercover officers on the kind of evidence they needed to collect.

Imagine a suspected paedophile talking about his abuse of a child. We don't have the child or children, or even know who they are. The undercover officer who is interacting with the suspect has to obtain as much detail about the alleged sexual assaults, the victim (or victims), the dates of offending, location, who else was present, who else he told, the weather, the time of day, what was on the news that day – anything that enables us to explore the crime with more precision and potentially corroborate that the assault took place. Because, given he was undercover, the officer must also satisfy a court that the suspect was not making up his answers to 'impress' another man he thought was a fellow paedophile.

The detectives were brutally frank in what we faced. Sexual abuse and paedophilia were spiralling out of control. In 1985 the Home Office had said there were 7,500 indecent images in circulation. In the early 2000s there were hundreds of thousands. By the time I retired, we had caught one person with two million indecent images. With the increasing availability and spread of the material, it wasn't something we could control. But by working pragmatically, we could at least control the way we approached the building of the cases.

As I worked with the Paedophile Unit and saw the extraordinary work they did, it reaffirmed my belief that the world of sub-committees, meetings and internal politics was distracting us from the important stuff, the fine detail that would allow us to make our prosecutions more successful. This, I knew, was about changing our procedures and adapting our thinking.

In the space of a few years, things had changed a great deal. I had long since abandoned my part-time career as a music promoter. There was no time for distractions now. I still had much to learn but being a prosecutor had gone way beyond being just a career. Having watched these cases up close, it was now all-consuming. I was unsure whether my own growth would count for much, though, unless the CPS grew too. Having now worked more closely with the police, I'd come to respect their public-facing outlook, so different to ours, and I wondered if it might be that same spirit which could make us more effective as an institution.

I thought back to the days when I'd sat in a classroom in Guildford learning law, watching the chalk skip along the blackboard as hoary shibboleths were handed down to a new generation of students. Back then, the law had seemed so contained, so straightforward, so easy to master. To have any chance of making a difference, I was going to have to unlearn much of what I had been taught.

IV

Tony Asciak's was one of the first faces I spotted whenever I made my way into court. He was a permanent fixture there, and always wore the same red tie with the same ill-fitting dark suit. You couldn't miss his large, round face glistening on the press bench. He had the look of a man who'd spent the night in a boozer until 3am. Everyone knew Tony.

He was something of a legend in Fleet Street circles and part of a long tradition of court reporting agencies that dated back to 1893. In 1976 he bought up the agency that specialised in covering the Magistrates' Courts in London, employing a small team to unearth national stories and bring them to the attention of the wider public in the media. Not much got past his team, and he was a true believer in the idea that these stories were not just entertainment: they were in the public interest.

'Morning Naz,' he said as I walked into court. He always called me Naz. 'Anything interesting on the list today?'

I would run through the latest serious robbery, murder and fraud cases, but Tony shook his head.

'No use to me. They'll end up in Crown Court and get covered by everybody,' he said. 'What I'm after are human stories. Ordinary people behaving badly and paying the consequences.'

I liked Tony from the moment I met him, and I also admired his honesty. I started to give him a heads up on cases that I felt deserved more attention from the public. Tony would rub his jowls and nod steadily as he worked out his angle. He told me what his readers would be interested in and over time, I began to learn the difference between what I thought was newsworthy and what the public wanted to hear.

'Think bigger than this place, Naz,' he said. 'Start to see yourself speaking directly to people at home.' These words resonated with me. I thought about the stories that we care about most, and what they tell us about ourselves. And then I started to wonder whether, by engaging the public in these stories, we might be able to involve them more in the process of justice. Could we get the public thinking differently about crime, and create change in our culture?

Although most of the cases I dealt with were traumatic, often bringing pain, suffering and loss to their victims, it wasn't unremittingly bleak. There was the occasional light moment, and Tony loved these too. Once, I mentioned in passing that a case on the list that day featured a couple who'd had sex on a train back from Margate to London. No one had complained as the two were observed in their act of passion on a crowded carriage. But witnesses did come forward and complain when the pair indulged in a relaxing post-coital cigarette. Smoking on a train was clearly a step too far.

When I told Tony this, his eyes gleamed. 'That's so British!' After he filed a piece on the story, everyone was talking about it: it was in every newspaper, and was even the subject of a Victoria Wood sketch.

Although some stories were more than a little frivolous, their popularity was such that they affirmed my idea that opening up what happened in a court to the wider public could be productive. Tony taught me more about advocacy than anything I learned in law school. He taught me that what I said in court could have an impact on the wider public. I had always thought that the future of the CPS couldn't just be about people like me doing my job, it had to be more about us involving the public in our work. One effective way to do this was by working with such reporters as Tony.

This was something that my colleagues often had quite different views on. For many of them, the idea of talking to someone who reported for the tabloids or mid-market dailies was taboo, probably because our profession was riddled with snobbery. But these media outlets had millions of readers and with that came enormous influence. To me, they offered far more potential for impact than our speaking only to the intelligentsia. Justice had to be for the many, not just for the gentlemen's club.

I began to take a bigger interest in the justice campaigns and interventions by the media that were shifting public opinion and helping create change. Not all of these were welcomed by my colleagues and some were more incendiary than others. But none could compete with the *Daily Mail*'s 1997 campaign to get justice for the family of the murdered black teenager Stephen Lawrence, knifed on a London street in 1993.

On 14 February, they ran a splash with the explosive headline 'Murderers!' under which were pictured the five suspects and a sub-heading simply stating: 'The Mail accuses these men of killing. If we are wrong, let them sue us'.

This was a huge risk for any newspaper to take, but the truth was on their side – and that headline said what we as prosecutors couldn't. All we could do was shuffle our feet. We were hamstrung by what the Lawrence Inquiry would later describe as 'a combination of professional incompetence, institutional racism and a failure of leadership by senior officers'. But the media weren't. They could see what was going on.

'These guys were taking the piss out of British justice,' said the editor at the time, Paul Dacre. And he was right.

That story had a huge impact and every prosecutor I knew welcomed it. The case was going cold and a shock was needed to revive it. I don't believe in trial by media, but there are indeed occasions when the media must intervene – and this was one of them. It would take a long time, but eventually we were able to secure prosecutions, leading to life sentences being handed down to two of Lawrence's killers. And it all started with that headline.

Then, on a slightly different note, there was the campaign to make changes to the Dangerous Dogs Act and stop dogs being needlessly condemned to death. This legislation had come into force in 1991 and meant that if someone was convicted for being in possession of a dangerous dog, the dog automatically had to be destroyed.

I had to prosecute a number of these cases and I struggled with the mandatory destruction section of the Act, which meant I was effectively sentencing dogs to death. In one case I convicted a police officer whose dog had escaped from a garage and bitten someone in the street. It wasn't a serious offence and yet the dog was put down. I found it upsetting, and I could also see the hurt it was causing many families. Dogs that weren't especially dangerous were being judged in the same way as violent breeds. There was no space for a judge's discretion or common sense. Several newspapers campaigned for this to change, so that the judges or magistrates could choose whether the dog should be destroyed depending on the circumstances, and I was relieved to see the law finally alter in 1997.

The law didn't always side with common sense or act in the best interests of the ordinary person. It was determined by elites, as it had always been, and was often hopelessly out of touch. Public pressure was the only thing that could force change, and the media had a valuable role in bringing the failings I was seeing on a daily basis to a much wider audience.

*

It wasn't just the law that the public needed to know a lot more about. I felt increasingly that the outdated attitudes we saw in court were impeding our work in other ways. In the court system, for example, everything revolved around the lawyers' timetable. The public were treated as an afterthought, even though justice was supposedly working on their behalf. Witnesses were informed they were required to turn up at court with barely any notice, sometimes only twenty-four hours. This was done without a thought for their childcare issues or work situation. 'The trial is fixed for tomorrow,' they'd be told. If a sixteen-year-old boy was required to give evidence in June, then he'd be required to turn up, even if he had school exams. There was no flexibility, no thought given to the real lives of the people affected by the law.

While the courts didn't pay any attention to the human lives of the people they were supposed to serve, I lost count of the number of times that a trial had to go part-heard and be finished another day to accommodate some social event on the part of the presiding judge or magistrate. I saw it happen all the time, but I didn't know how to change the culture.

I was particularly concerned about the victims of crime. They were treated as a commodity and this was reflected in the language used to describe them. Police officers, barristers and judges all spoke in the same way: 'Which victim shall we *use* to present the case?' they might ask. It was far too easy for them to forget the person behind it all.

Inside the court itself, there was often precious little empathy. Victims would be forced to stand outside court with the suspect's family, or defendants and witnesses were placed close together. The court should have tried to mitigate such intensely stressful situations, but there was always a victim a few chairs away from someone who had ruined their life. There is no doubt in my mind that one of the reasons that many witnesses were reluctant to come to court was the hostile environment they faced there, not to mention that after giving evidence in such cases, there was very rarely any aftercare or trauma counselling either. It hurt me to see people suffering and I knew I wasn't doing enough. I was so busy, I just moved on to the next person to let down.

I knew that systemic change wouldn't happen overnight, but I thought that sunshine was the best disinfectant and the more light shone on our profession, the better for us all. When I was approached by the BBC regarding a drama they were planning about prosecutors, I wondered whether it might be the opportunity I had been looking for. Perhaps because they knew I had an interest in working with the public, my bosses put me forward to work with Nick Collins on the show. When I learned that *Crown Prosecutor* was to star Michael Praed of *Dynasty* and *Robin of Sherwood* fame, I assumed they had a big budget. How wrong I was. Ten episodes of thirty minutes were written for BBC One Drama with an inexpensive cast and an even cheaper set in East

London, in the former Old Truman Brewery. Everything was done on a shoestring. At least that was realistic, I thought, my mind on our own budget cuts.

Nick drew heavily from my casework to develop his scripts and he would send Michael down to my office in Victoria to observe me in action. Michael was a handsome man and I had never been so popular among my female colleagues as I was then. I went to the set to consult, and Michael called me whenever he had a question: should he stand up in court, or sit down? That kind of thing. One day he rang while I was driving, so I pulled over to answer. Once I'd told him whatever information it was that he needed to know, I looked behind me on the hard shoulder to see a police car parked. There was a knock on my window.

'Is everything OK, sir?' an officer asked, as I lowered the glass.

'Yes, thank you,' I replied.

'The hard shoulder is for emergencies only.'

'I know, it was an emergency call,' I said. 'A court case that needed my immediate attention.' Perhaps the creative licence had rubbed off on me.

In the run up to its first broadcast, we were all very excited that the CPS was about to raise its profile. The first episode got eight million viewers, which by today's standards was pretty good. But it bombed spectacularly and the reviews were excoriating. 'The dialogue makes *Crossroads* seem like Flaubert,' said the *Independent*. The series 'looked like a badly acted employment training video,' noted the *Guardian*. 'BBC1's stolid refutation of the adage that "you can't go wrong with courtroom drama" finally hit the screens last night and I for one would like to say thank you, thank you for a bloody good laugh,' wrote Lynne Truss in *The Times*. The viewing figures fell week by week and eventually, the BBC quietly announced there would be no follow-up series. It was not quite what I had hoped, or expected, from the CPS's public debut. If anything, it made us look worse. I would have to find a new way of approaching public engagement.

The ratings for the TV drama may not have been high, but the government was watching the CPS. In 1997, the Attorney General ordered a review, which was highly critical of its performance while acknowledging the challenges that were holding us back. It confirmed that we were under-resourced and that many of our staff had inadequate training and were also under too much pressure. It concluded that we were failing in our mission. Different working practices and a new culture needed to be introduced for the CPS to find its rightful place in the criminal justice system.

'The government fully accept the need for change in the CPS,' announced Attorney General John Morris, presenting the report to Parliament. 'We intend to lose no time in starting the process.' After the government's critical review of the CPS, Dame Barbara Mills announced that she would be standing down as Director of Public Prosecutions, to be replaced by

David Calvert-Smith, who quickly secured a significant 25 per cent increase in funding from the government.

We were still struggling to build the public confidence in us, however. And even though we were slowly becoming a more diverse organisation in some ways, we remained far too remote from the public. I was realising that to make the kind of cultural change I wanted and to reach the public properly, I would have to go out and meet them and see how things were happening on the ground.

At the turn of the millennium, social tensions were high on the streets of Britain, and I knew from my own experiences that there were entire communities with whom the police had no contact. It was in these places that crime thrived, and that victims had little access to anything approaching real justice. Like my dad before me, I knew the value of working with local communities and I was regularly meeting with charities and voluntary groups in London. One of the crimes that worried me most, and that seemed to be growing at an alarming rate, was gang-related violence. I wanted to understand why carrying knives was becoming a norm for teenagers and when in 2001 I was approached by Kola Williams, a former gang member in Harlesden, North London, I hoped he would be able to tell me more.

Kola carried a bullet in his thigh, a reminder of the dangers of his gangland past, and was articulate and passionate about steering kids away from crime. He ran a community centre and club called NW10 and had been trying to work with Brent police, but for reasons that weren't entirely clear to me, they didn't have a good relationship. I wondered if I might be able to help change that. I figured that if I worked with him this could be a backdoor to building credibility with the police, and that he might also start to trust the CPS and police more.

I had been asking my staff for some time to engage more with young people and their default response was always to invite teenage groups to our offices. Because our environment was alien to them, they of course rarely came. Maybe, I thought, we should go to them.

I suggested this to Kola, and he arranged a meet up above a bookies near his club. It was their safe environment. I told police of my plans and was warned not to go, as the site had been risk assessed and deemed dangerous. But we had to take some risks if we were ever going to build bridges and understand what was happening in our communities. Besides, Kola had reassured me that he would provide security, and I trusted him.

I arrived one early evening to find thirty or so teenagers, with their faces covered so I couldn't identify them. Kola introduced me and I looked out at the sea of colourful bandanas, eager to get to know the people behind the masks.

'My job is to keep you safe, not just lock you up if you commit a crime,' I told them.

I wanted to understand why knives were so important to them and, when I asked if they were carrying, they all nodded or raised a fist. 'Me too,' I responded, pulling out my car keys, which had a tiny pocketknife attached. They laughed at this and one of them reached into his jacket, pulling out a 12-inch knife and waving it in the air.

'You win!' I said, laughing uncertainly.

I now had their attention. I told them that the IRA had murdered a family member and that I was from a community that had felt they could expect nothing from the police. I could see that everyone in the room was listening.

We talked at length about their problems with the police, stop and search, poverty, poor education and lack of opportunities to get on. I could see that in many ways, their environment was an incubator for crime.

What struck me straight away was the intense hostility they felt towards Brent police. They were angry that the police had refused to meet them on the basis that they were gang members. As far as they were concerned, the police had determined they were criminals so couldn't possibly help them. They had been written off, and there was a cavernous gap between them and the authorities that seemed to be widening by the day.

They also talked about the estates where they lived, and painted a picture of chronic council neglect. They felt abandoned by the authorities. They told me their street lighting didn't work and that the council refused to rehouse people, or carry out any repairs on council homes. They told me crack dens were operating in open sight and, most of the time, the police tolerated them. Every now and then there would be a big, over-the-top raid and the territorial support group would charge in at six in the morning. Doors would be smashed down and helicopters would circle overhead, and the police would be accompanied by a minibus of councillors and local community leaders to show them that they were on top of crime. Within twenty-four hours the crack den would have relocated and be operating again.

I also heard how these young people didn't get the chance to sit exams at school. It seemed everyone had written them off as troublemakers, and they were failed by the system on so many levels. It quickly became clear to me they wanted to get on, but felt trapped. There was an earnestness and desperation to their voices, but nobody was listening to them. Understanding their anger, after an hour I promised them that I would act upon what they had told me.

I went to see the head of the interpersonal violence team at the Home Office and asked if any research had been carried out by government into why young men were carrying knives. He looked at me quizzically and shook his head.

'Don't you think it would be a good idea?' I asked, explaining what issues had come up in the conversation I'd had with that group of young men. 'This community should have the opportunity to explain their circumstances and what's going wrong.'

He responded with the police default position that it wasn't advisable to talk to criminals.

'Well, how else are we going to find out the causes of crime if we don't talk to them?' I asked. He acknowledged that I had a point and said the Home Office were starting a conversation around this, and were looking to create a Serious Violent Crime Strategy.

When I argued that this strategy should be informed by young people like those I met in Brent, he agreed. I gave him Kola's details and he was one of many who were invited to group discussions that the Home Office set up to establish the government's first ever Serious Violent Crime Strategy a few years later.

By now, I was fortunate to be on an upward trajectory. In 2001, at thirty-eight years old, I was the youngest person and the first Muslim to be appointed Assistant Chief Crown Prosecutor for London. I had also remarried, several years after my divorce, and was truly happy at home too. Two years later, I would become Director of Prosecutions for London. More than ever, I looked to the public to see what justice needed to look like. And now people were starting to look to me. I would soon be able to help set the agenda for a new era in British law.

V

Now that I had established myself in the CPS, I was able to give more thought to cultural change, and the personal passions that had always driven me. There was a particular social issue, one which very often resulted in tragic consequences, that I knew would become a focus for me. I called it gender terrorism.

I had witnessed the realities of sexism for myself. When I was young, I had noticed that my sister would walk ten yards behind me on the way to school. When I asked her why, she told me it was because everyone else did the same. She'd learned that males must lead and females follow. Even as a child, I knew this was wrong. When I looked around the streets, I realised she was simply copying others. Men in my community would walk six or seven paces in front of their wife, sister or daughter. It was something I saw constantly. This would present the odd situation where occasionally I would see two men chatting and two women behind them, who would come together and talk. When the men parted company the two women would immediately assume their positions, following the men ten yards behind.

It seemed bizarre to me, particularly because in my own household my mother had always sought to empower girls. Even though my family hailed from a 'traditional' patriarchal culture, I could never accept that women should be controlled by men, and that had certainly never been the case in my own home.

Through my mother's battles with our neighbours, I had learned about forced marriage, and seen first-hand Mum's fight to change this culture. I watched her argue with men who tried to stop their wives from learning to drive, because they were apprehensive of the freedom it would give them; on one occasion she intervened when a man beat his wife because he discovered she had taken a driving lesson. These were passionate, angry exchanges and I hung on every word. And I knew Mum was right.

My sense of this injustice became stronger as I got older, especially as I saw how powerfully enshrined it was in cultural traditions. I was invited to various first birthday parties, an important milestone in Sikh, Hindu and Islamic culture. They were often lavish. But they were always only for boys.

Once I attended two Sikh friends' first birthday party for their son and I couldn't help but notice they also had a two-year-old daughter. I asked why they hadn't held a party for her.

'It's different for boys,' the father said. Daughters, they added, were a burden.

I was shocked, of course, but throughout my adult life, I repeatedly heard that phrase. *Daughters are a burden.* Fathers would shrug and tell me their job was to bring up their daughters then marry them off – and they'd have to pay a dowry to do this. After this, the daughters would no longer be their responsibility. This entrenched attitude was why forced marriage at a young age was so popular; the older a daughter got without being married off, the greater the likelihood she would make her own choices. And that was not acceptable. Sons were seen as a family's security, carer, protection. Daughters, on the other hand, were thought of, and treated, as possessions.

Mum's attitude certainly rubbed off on me and over the years, I became more forceful in challenging these attitudes whenever I encountered them.

Once, at a wedding, an acquaintance bemoaned his terrible year: a son had gone to prison for drug dealing but, even worse, his daughter had decided she wanted to marry someone of her own choice!

'Can you believe that? What shame she brings to our family,' he sighed. He continued this anguished diatribe for a few minutes, until I interjected, suggesting that perhaps it was his son who had brought shame on the family.

I had countless conversations like this, as well as those with people who would talk to me only about their sons and act as though their daughters didn't exist.

'My son is growing into a fine young man, Nazir. He's

working so hard at school,' they would tell me, their eyes shining with pride.

'But you've got three daughters,' I replied. 'What about them?'

The worst of these conversations took place at another wedding reception with a young Sikh man. Born, raised and educated in the UK, he was twenty-one years old. Apropos of nothing, he started to talk to me about women.

'Man is like gold,' he said, 'and woman is like silk.'

At first, I thought this sounded rather poetic.

'And here's the thing,' he continued. 'If you drop a piece of gold in mud you can pick it out, wipe it clean and it's as good as new. But if you drop silk in mud . . .' he paused, looking me directly in the eye, 'then it's stained forever.' I told him, astonished, that his view was idiotic.

I always challenged these views, but I'm ashamed to say there was one occasion when I failed to do so. And it came as I walked the corridors of North Middlesex University Hospital in June 1996. I say 'walked', but at the time I was floating on air, filled with joy. It was moments after the first of my four children was born. I had just left my wife in the delivery suite and had rushed out to call my nearest and dearest to tell them how proud I was to be the father of a daughter.

Within seconds my euphoria had melted into anguish.

'It's a girl,' I said excitedly into the phone, only to hear silence at the other end.

'Oh, I'm sorry,' came the response. 'Better luck next time.'

The same conversation has played out in my mind many times and I am still disgusted at myself because I didn't challenge it. I was too tired, shocked and disappointed to react.

The truth is, however, that this idiotic view is the world's oldest prejudice. In Greek mythology Pandora, the first woman, was created as a punishment to mark the end of paradise for men. It was she who released evil into the world and ended the Golden Age of man. Writing in the sixth century BCE, the Ancient Greek poet Hipponax wrote, 'two days are sweetest for a woman, the day a man marries her and the day he carries her out dead.' Aristotle famously – or perhaps infamously – wrote that by nature, women were 'inferior'. Then think of Eve, too, in the garden of Eden, succumbing to temptation. Misogyny has deep roots in every religion and culture, from Islamic patriarchal traditions of the kind I had witnessed in my own community to Christian fundamentalism.

Of course, as a man I couldn't ever possibly truly understand the unbearable horror this caused for women, many of whom feared for their safety and even their lives. I could at least educate myself on what was happening, however. I knew femicide was occurring on an industrial scale across the globe. Millions of infant girls across Asia were being aborted, killed, fatally neglected and abandoned, solely because their parents had wanted a son. Meanwhile, girls and women were being brutally murdered around the world in so-called 'honour killings' because they had supposedly behaved inappropriately, bringing shame on the family name and so, to use the idiotic silk analogy, become 'stained forever'.

In the year 2000, the United Nations estimated that 5,000 women were victims of honour killings every year. I knew this was nonsense, a figure plucked out of the air. You only had to do the most basic of research or listen to what women's groups were saying to realise the real figure was much, much higher. More than that were being killed in Pakistan alone. Women were being poisoned, shot, stabbed, strangled, set on fire, butchered, subjected to acid attacks and stoned to death all over the world. And the executions were always appallingly brutal – one stab wound or bullet was never enough. Girls would be stabbed up to a hundred times or riddled with bullets in front of young witnesses. Why? To send a message to other women and girls. This will happen to you if you do not stay in line. Do as we say, or the same fate awaits you.

These same concerns preoccupied me in my work as well, because we had started to see such cases coming to light in Britain. Around this time, world leaders were busy pursuing a global 'war on terror' but there was one brutal act that continued to be ignored. Hardly anyone spoke of this gender terrorism.

In the summer of 2003, I had recently been appointed the Director of Prosecutions for London and was standing in the office of my boss, the new Director of Public Prosecutions, Ken Macdonald. We discussed honour killings and I explained that I had a postbag full of correspondence from victims and survivors' groups asking me to explore the issue. There and then he gave me the go-ahead to get out and focus on the kind of work that I knew needed to be done. I had his full support. Emboldened by my new role, I started to set up meetings.

First, I met Jasvinder Sanghera, the founder of Karma Nirvana – a charity that supports people affected by honour-based violence and forced marriages – and Southall Black Sisters, a long-established advocacy service working to challenge gender-related violence against women. The stories they told me, as they explained how honour-based violence was increasing, were chilling, More and more victims were suffering at the hands of criminals who had no fear of punishment, as many of their crimes were able to pass under the radar.

There had been a small number of prosecutions for these cases in the past but, as I reviewed the material, I realised we were ill-equipped to deal with the unique realities of this particular crime. We treated these cases like any other kind of homicide, when in fact their handling was often infused with the same kind of sexism that had created this horrific culture.

I began by looking at the 1999 murder of Rukhsana Naz, a nineteen-year-old from Derbyshire who was strangled by her mother and brother after she refused to have an abortion. I also reviewed the murder of Heshu Yones, a sixteen-year-old from West London who had her throat slit by her father after she started dating an eighteen-year-old Lebanese student. In both cases, successful prosecutions were made, but it was clear to me that the justice system hadn't really begun to grapple with the complex nature of the crime. In Yones's case, she was portrayed as wayward and when the judge came to sentencing, he even said he understood what it must be like to have a daughter who was out of control. The killer got a reduced tariff as a result. This embodied a toxic mindset, one that had to be challenged.

I knew that more time needed to be devoted to exploring the issues underlying the crime, so set about organising what was to be the world's first major conference on honour-based violence and forced marriage. I booked a conference room in a hotel in Westminster, expecting only a small group of experts to attend. But, to my delight, we were completely overwhelmed by attendees. Survivors, victims, civil servants, police, policy makers, social workers and women's groups came in their droves, as well as international media. And everyone, wherever they came from, wanted to lay claim to having a deep history of honour-based violence. The Italian delegates argued that they invented honour violence and referred to the Capulets and Montagues defending their family name, while the French said their history pre-dated that through duelling at dawn. Nevertheless, we were all agreed on one thing. It had always been about power and control and, in that respect, nothing had changed.

I listened to some powerful stories that day. The most powerful of all was Jasvinder Sanghera's. An inspirational woman and campaigner, Jasvinder had run away to escape a forced marriage as a teenager. She had seen her older sisters forced into marriage at a young age and one of her sisters tragically died from self-immolation after she was abused by her husband.

So when, as a fourteen-year-old, Jasvinder was shown a photograph of a man and told she had to marry him, as she had been promised to him from the age of eight, she knew what horrors may lie ahead. She refused. She was taken out of education and locked in a room, held prisoner by her parents. They brought food to the door and told her she wouldn't be released until she agreed to the marriage.

In the end she reluctantly said yes, but only so she could plan her escape. She fled from Derby to Newcastle and never looked back, later starting a charity from her kitchen table to help others in the same position. Jasvinder quickly became one of the most knowledgeable voices in the country on honour-based violence, and it was a privilege to be able to speak to her on the subject.

'Today was fantastic,' she told me. 'But you have to keep going, Nazir. This is just the beginning.'

Jasvinder began to share case studies of victims of honour-based violence she had supported, helping to give us a better picture of where potential hotspots were for these crimes. London, the West Midlands, West Yorkshire, Lancashire and Manchester were high-risk areas, but Jasvinder and her charity Karma Nirvana never turned any potential victim away, regardless of where they were located. Most had fled their homes and sought accommodation miles away from their families. Karma Nirvana had struggled to get support from a multitude of agencies who just didn't understand the dynamics of honour-based abuse.

Several authorities, when approached by the family of the victim, were unaware that mediation was not an option. Families were prepared to say anything to ensure that the victim was returned to them. They would suggest mental illness had caused the victim to run away or 'misinterpret' (the families' word) their intentions. Too often the authorities, in their ignorance and their desire to close the case, were quick to arrange the victim's return to their family, especially if she was still legally a child. The fact that the victim's horrifying situation was now going to worsen was something they chose not to recognise.

Many of these victims were dispatched by their families to their countries of origin, never to be seen again, a significant number undoubtedly meeting a tragic and unnecessary death, some through taking their own lives – something that cannot be seen as suicide when it was surely driven by the actions of their families. Many others will have surely been murdered, extinguished from existence without any consequences for those who did it.

By now, I had enough material gathered to get the government involved. I spoke to the Head of the Interpersonal Violence Team at the Home Office and explained we needed a cross-government response to this issue. He listened carefully and acted promptly, organising a round table that brought together senior civil servants from government departments and senior figures from the CPS along with Commander Steve Allen, who was to become the Association of Chief Police Officers' lead on honour-based violence and forced marriage.

What quickly became apparent in our discussions was that no one had any coherent data on this crime, so Steve agreed to get data analysts at the Met to go through all homicides that took place across the country in 2005 and see if there were any cases where honour might have played a part in the killings. A few months later, having interrogated the data, we learned that in that year at least twelve people in the UK had been murdered in an honour crime.

It was a sobering starting point, but we knew this wasn't the full figure as there were also girls being exported for murder. Girls were being taken back to Pakistan, Bangladesh, India and other countries, never to return. Then there were the girls reported missing in the UK who were never found. There had been a successful prosecution in one of these cases: Shafilea Ahmed in Warrington was one girl we did manage to find. She was reported missing by her parents in September 2003 and there had been a nationwide hunt to find her. Her body was eventually discovered the following February in a river in Cumbria, but the CPS was only able to prosecute her parents years later, when Shafilea's younger sister bravely came forward and told police that her father had killed her.

Murders were not the only kinds of honour crimes; there

was physical and emotional violence and sexual abuse. And there was another group I was worried we weren't considering. From conversations with Southall Black Sisters, I learned that suicide, resulting from fear of honour-based violence, was also something we needed to consider. One harrowing case had stuck in my mind, that of a young Sikh woman who had jumped in front of a train in Southall with her two young children. Navjeet Sidhu was twenty-seven years old, pregnant and in an unhappy arranged marriage when she jumped in front of a 100mph Heathrow Express train with her five-year-old daughter and twenty-three-month-old son.

The inquest heard that family pressure had led to Navjeet's suicide and that her husband had refused to help. Southall Black Sisters knew that she had been seeking advice in the weeks before her death and felt certain her suicide was linked to her unhappy marriage. But it was difficult to bring together the evidence that might prove this.

I thought about ways we might be able to gather meaningful data on such deaths, and eventually asked the British Transport Police if they could look into rail suicides to see what they might be able to find. They agreed to do some research and came back to me to say that, while they couldn't provide exact figures on whether suicides might be honour related, a third of rail suicides for the year 2005–6 took place on the Great Western line between Southall and Slough. This was immediately interesting to me because of the demography of the area, which is sizeably South Asian. And when

we looked deeper into the figures it showed a disproportionately high number of fatalities were women of Asian origin.
The data was showing what I'd suspected all along. That gender terrorism in the UK was a growing trend, and that lives
were at stake if we continued not to act.

If we were going to bring it to justice in a court of law, we
needed a clearer, accepted definition of honour-based abuse. I
brought together a dozen women's groups to help with this,
which in turn led to an ACPO (Association of Chief Police
Officers) definition of honour-based violence, as 'a crime or
incident, which has or may have been committed to protect or
defend the honour of the family and/or community'. Now we
had a definition, we were in a much stronger position when it
came to tackling the crime.

Commander Steve Allen issued this new definition to
forces along with guidance on how to provide a proactive
response to those affected by honour-based violence. He
also oversaw moves to ensure police authorities around the
country had specialist officers to make victims, or potential
victims, as safe as possible, supporting whatever decision
they took and pointing them to sources of support. We also
agreed that specialist prosecutors needed to be in place in
every county, and that they should liaise with specialist leads
in each force.

In achieving this, we had laid the foundations for improve-
ments in the prosecution of these cases. Prosecutions were

happening more frequently, and we were getting better not just at dealing with UK-based honour crimes but also cases where people had been taken abroad to be murdered. One of these featured Surjit Athwal, a twenty-six-year-old customs officer at Heathrow, who was murdered after she had an affair with a colleague and asked her husband for a divorce. She'd been in an unhappy arranged marriage since she was sixteen years old.

Surjit's family meticulously planned her murder and she was lured to the Punjab in India for a family wedding. Once there, her grandmother's brother strangled her and dumped her body in the River Ravi. Her husband attempted to cover up the crime by forging letters to the Indian authorities, but we managed to make convictions thanks to the help of Surjit's brother Jagdeesh who ran a one-man campaign to keep Surjit on everyone's radar. Surjit's husband and grandmother subsequently received life sentences. I would meet the grandmother in prison, on a visit to talk to inmates, and when she saw me, she shouted in Punjabi. It may not have been a language I spoke well, but I recognised the insults. I also knew that all that mattered to her was that back in India, she was considered a heroine. She didn't care if she was going to be locked up in a jail for twenty-five years. That chilled me. When people are totally blind to the evil they commit, and serious crimes become not just normalised but seen as *heroic* acts, then we are losing the battle. Justice cannot work without remorse, or the acknowledgement that crimes were just that.

I had seriously underestimated the emotional pull of the honour code. It wasn't enough to get better at prosecuting the people who committed these crimes, or to try and reason logically with perpetrators. We'd only be able to start winning this war once we treated honour crimes differently to others. We had to start looking at this as a kind of organised crime. It was just like dealing with the mafia: the honour code able to dissolve the strongest bonds of love and create violent hatred. One case brought this home to me more than any other: that of Samaira Nazir.

In 2000, the nineteen-year-old caught sight of a young man as he entered her family store in Southall Broadway, West London. Salman Mohammed was an asylum seeker who had fled Afghanistan and smuggled himself into Britain in the back of a lorry. As he talked to Samaira's brother, Azhar, who would go on to help him find lodgings and a job, he caught sight of Samaira. The two exchanged awkward smiles and from this chance meeting, feelings of love began to blossom and they began a forbidden relationship.

Several years later, Samaira's parents took her to Pakistan to meet potential suitors for an arranged marriage but on her return she told her parents it was pointless. She couldn't go through with it. She loved someone else, she told them, and wanted to marry him. She may as well have told them she had joined a devil-worshipping cult for the reaction it provoked. At 10am the next morning, her mother went with Samaira to see her boyfriend and pleaded with the pair of them to end their relationship, but they refused. They were in love, and they wanted her permission to get married.

Her mother buried her face in her hands. 'I beg you not to do this. If you do, I don't know what will happen.'

Two hours later, Samaira was stabbed eighteen times, brutally murdered by her seventeen-year-old cousin Imran Mohammed in the presence of two infant nieces who were splattered with her blood.

The police had been building their case ever since, and we sat down to discuss the prosecution. In this instance we suspected that Imran had been chosen as the killer because he had the least to lose, and so had been instructed to do it by others in the family. It would be easy to prosecute him because he was covered in her blood and he had confessed to the crime. However, this was what the family wanted. We knew there was a wider web of guilt, but it was hard to prove it.

My mind went back to the idea that honour crime was almost like mafia crime. We had to break the '*omertà*', the code of silence. We knew the people involved would not talk, so authority was given to deploy covert listening devices in Samaira's family house. The police initially put a listening device in the goldfish tank and then arranged for 'trigger events', in the form of a televised press conference or high-profile community meeting, to get the family talking. It worked. We recorded conversations that told us exactly what we had suspected. We heard Azhar and his father tell others to keep quiet, saying that it didn't matter if Imran was convicted. It gave us enough circumstantial evidence to arrest both of them.

Nevertheless, the findings were extremely troubling to me, because all the evidence suggested that Azhar had been truly close to his sister. How did he go from that to being party to her murder?

It was yet another poisonous example of what the honour code did to people. Doubtless he would have been told that Samaira's marriage to Salman would be the most shameful thing that could happen to their family, and this notion of shame would have been instilled in him from a young age. That is what made a brother who genuinely loved his sister arrange her murder and persuade his cousin to carry out the act. Hard to fathom and utterly senseless, this was what we were up against.

When the case came to trial at the Old Bailey, the court heard how Azhar had joined in the assault with Imran, stabbing his sister repeatedly in a prolonged and frenzied attack. This, too, had been obtained through a covert listening device. Azhar's two daughters, aged two and four, had been forced to watch as they cut her throat. Her father, who had also been charged, fled to Pakistan while on bail and to my frustration escaped justice and died there. God got him before I could. But Samaira's brother and cousin were jailed for life.

It was to be a seminal case, both changing how the police approached honour killings and giving us a strategy for dealing with them. We had to treat them like the organised, networked killings that they were, intended both to punish and to send a message to others: do as we say, or you're next. Steve Allen and I discussed this at length, and he agreed to update his police guidance notes for squads across the country in the light of Samaira's case and impress on the police the need to treat honour crime as *organised* crime.

We were no longer chasing individual killers. We had to smash networks, capture conspirators and break the cultural cover. We weren't going to let one sacrificial lamb be held responsible for these brutal acts: I wanted everyone involved put behind bars. But even though progress was being made in the courts, it was clear that as a nation we were still struggling to get to grips with these crimes and how we talk about them.

Throughout the Samaira Nazir case Channel 4 were given near total access to our investigation. They had asked to follow a case from start to finish, and we allowed them to film everything, including conferences with the police and our strategic discussions on how we would get beyond the wall of silence. We had never given anyone this level of access to such an investigation before, and were therefore surprised to get a call as soon as the trial finished saying that the film would not be broadcast. Was the subject matter too inflammatory, I asked, to no avail. Their decision remains a mystery to this day.

Certainly, I knew there were many who didn't want to believe honour crimes were happening every day in Britain. And the full horror of what was occurring was only just beginning to register properly with the public at large. But politicians were also struggling to speak about the issue. For years they had taken great pride in our multicultural society, ignoring the fact that in choosing separatism over universality we were following a recipe for disaster. We had become a society that focused on difference, and not what we share. Of course I was in favour of multiculturalism – and I believe my family showed how integration could work, and how immigration could bring so much to a nation. But we could not tolerate those traditions that threatened to hurt members of the community. I learned that as a young boy, watching my mother hold court around the kitchen table.

Instead of building stronger bonds, we were creating a permissive environment where it was deemed normal to turn a blind eye to honour crimes, forced marriage and female genital mutilation in the name of cultural sensitivity. Somewhere in this multicultural haze, we had lost sight of the fact that we were denying women their basic human rights, the right to an education, to a childhood. The right to sexual pleasure, the right to marry when, and whom, they wanted and the right to leave a relationship that has failed, or is abusive.

The truth was simple: the rights of the vulnerable, of children, women and all of us, individually must always trump the demands of any culture.

As I looked back on the Samaira Nazir case, I couldn't help but think of all the women and girls we didn't know about. For every prosecution we made, there were surely countless others where criminals had escaped justice. Details of cases shared with me by NGOs forever preyed on my mind. Like the story of an Iraqi girl getting married in Britain with blood pouring from her nose: it was a forced marriage and she was beaten just moments before the ceremony. Incredibly, the Imam continued. Or the story of six-year-old Alisha Begum, the youngest victim of honour killing in Britain. She died after two men set fire to her house, to warn her brother off a relationship with a woman of whom the two men didn't approve.

If I allowed myself to dwell, these horrors would flash in my mind. I had wanted more knowledge of these crimes, but now I had it, it sometimes felt as though I knew too much. There was still so much to be done, too: while new guidelines had been issued, no police force in England or Wales was yet formally recording honour crimes. Then there was the question of those cultural beliefs, which I knew would always be so hard to change. I suspected we would experience a lot more bloodshed.

VI

I've never shied away from tough conversations. And when dealing with issues that others might be afraid to talk about, this has come to be a help. As uncomfortable as it can be to speak to someone and see intense pain, anger or confusion in their eyes, it's often from such exchanges that you learn the most. I have stood before grieving parents, unapologetic criminals and victims who have suffered unimaginable loss and, no matter how difficult and testing those times were, I always came away knowing and understanding more.

After the London terror attacks in 2005, in which fifty-two people were killed and over seven hundred injured, some of these conversations – particularly those involving 'culturally sensitive' topics – became increasingly challenging. The police had identified the murderers as four radical British Islamists and, as tensions were high, I knew that the risk of hate crime was very real. I wanted to get out and talk to the Muslim community, to show that we were engaging with them and to allay any fears they might have. A national roadshow was arranged, with the first public event taking place at City Hall. I was joined by Sue Hemming, then head of our Counter Terrorism Prosecution Team, and we began to speak about the challenge of extremism and why hate crime wouldn't be tolerated: the Muslim community could not, and should not, be held responsible for the actions of those terrorists. Speaking from the small stage, I looked out at faces filled with worry.

'But we all have to be vigilant,' I said. 'There are extremists in every city and we have to root out this cancer, challenge their poisonous narratives.'

'I disagree,' said a voice loudly from the audience. 'It's not our responsibility. That's the job of the police.'

'He's right,' replied another voice. 'What can we do about it? Let's tell it how it is. This is because of British foreign policy. Our government has radicalised Muslims.'

I disagreed with this perspective. The 9/11 attacks in New York came after the UK and America had intervened to protect Muslims from being slaughtered in places including the former Yugoslavia and, while there were certainly global tensions as a result, this was no excuse for using Islam to further the violent agendas of terrorists by attacking civilians going about their daily lives.

'Don't for one second think these people are Koranic soldiers,' I said. 'Nothing about them is faithful to Islam.'

These tense conversations often lasted for hours, but I understood why people were so afraid. I was also desperately worried about how susceptible to radicalisation our young people were, and how easily they could be brainwashed. Much of the vulnerability of British Muslims came from insecurities about their identity, with many feeling they had neither any sense of British identity nor real stake in society – and this was everyone's problem.

I also felt that there was an intersection here with the extreme attitudes to gender that were so destructive in parts of the British Asian community (though it should be said that the effects of misogyny can be felt and seen across all communities in Britain). In the honour crime cases that now piled up on my desk, what I realised was that some young British Asian women had little to no access to the rights we assumed everyone in Britain enjoyed. These women may have been living in Britain, but they could have been holed up in the most feudal and repressive part of Afghanistan. Theirs was not a world where they could listen to music, go to university, choose a career or date whoever they wanted. Theirs was a world where they could never realise their potential. Theirs was a world where they were expected to suffer in silence and if they so much as stepped a millimetre out of line, they could face the most brutal and sickening punishment imaginable.

Now my eyes were trained on the issue, I saw this tyranny wherever I went. On one occasion I was introduced to a young woman at a community event who, I noticed, was wearing her wedding ring on the ring finger of her right hand rather than on the conventional left. As we talked, I grew curious about why she wore it this way and eventually asked her. She was quiet for a long time and when she looked up and spoke, her voice was defiant. 'I do this because I was forced to marry my husband.' She had precious little power, so this was the only way she could protest.

In October 2005, a young British-Iraqi Kurdish woman stepped into a South London police station to make a report about her treatment at the hands of her husband. Her dark hair was tied back in a bun, a few loose strands framing her face, and she wore fashionably ripped jeans and a sweater. She fidgeted nervously with some papers in her hands, and her hazel eyes blinked in the electric light of the small interview room. Her name was Banaz Mahmod.

Banaz was twenty years old, from South London. She was trying to build a life for herself, like any other young woman. But there was one thing that set her apart. She was fighting the tyranny of the honour code, and she knew she could be killed for it. In summoning the courage to step into that police interview room, Banaz was about to expose powerfully both the failings of British justice and the pitiful inadequacy of our response to this crime.

In the remarkable police videotape of that interview, you can hear her voice trembling as she begins to tell a police officer about her husband.

'He was a strict husband,' she said. 'Whenever he wanted to have sex, it was just his way, always his way. Whenever I said no, he wouldn't take no for an answer, he would just start raping me.' She had been seventeen when she was married against her will. 'I tried to stop him, but he just slapped me or hit me on the back or pulled me by the hair. That's when he said to me he would kill me if I said anything to anyone.'

Banaz paused for a second and even in the grainy videotape it is clear for anyone to see how hard it was for her to compose herself. She thought it was normal to be treated this way, she said. I was particularly struck by one of her recollections on the tape: once, when the couple had guests at their home, Banaz had called her husband by his first name. In her culture, to do this in public was not permitted. 'After the guests left,' she continued on the video, 'he told me that if I called him by his name the next time, he would stick a knife in me.'

Banaz's husband became increasingly violent, and she now experienced memory loss from having been repeatedly brutally beaten by him. She had kept the extent of her suffering from her family, but when her sister discovered the truth, she told Banaz's parents, who confronted Ali.

Ali admitted that he beat their daughter, but said it was because she was disrespectful and Banaz's parents agreed that she must try harder to be a better wife. Whenever she went back to her parents' home from that day onwards, she said, they told her she needed to go back to him, and try harder to please him.

On the tape, she leans forward and nervously folds her fingers into her palm, clenching her fists. 'I was brainwashed,' she said. But a couple of months afterwards, she added, she

113

had come to a realisation. 'I made up my mind that I wanted a divorce.' She told her mother, packed up some of her things, and left.

In the video, she swallows hard and wipes her eyes. In making this choice, Banaz knew she had put herself in grave danger. Her family were never going to agree to the dishonour of a divorce.

After leaving her husband, Banaz met another man, Rahmat. They started a friendship, which quickly grew into a relationship. They fell in love. The pair hoped for a future together, free from the repressive culture that wouldn't allow her, or them, to be happy. But Banaz's family was never going to let this happen. They were culturally bound to do everything they could to oppose it. In Iraq, a woman can be murdered by a hired hitman for as little as $100. Women who commit adultery are frequently stoned to death and the authorities rarely intervene. These strict tribal customs are, in fact, openly celebrated.

Banaz knew the danger her choices had put her in. Every time she stepped out into the street in London, she knew she would be under constant surveillance. Dozens of eyes would be upon her, tracking her every move. Young men in her community, cousins and extended family members, would all be watching her, following her – and she knew they had been sent by her husband. Once, a car pulled up beside her and some men told her to get inside. She refused and on that occasion managed to get away, but the surveillance continued.

Her stalkers saw her embrace Rahmat outside Morden tube station and, as the two of them kissed, the men scurried away to tell her family. And that's when a 'family war council' of men was convened. They decided that, for bringing shame on the family, Banaz must die.

In the interview room in South London, the police officer sat unmoved as Banaz told her that she needed help, because these men continued to follow her. 'In the future or at any time, if anything happens to me, it's them,' she said. 'Now that I'm giving this statement what can you do for me?' she pleaded.

Watching the video made me emotional. The police officer should have realised the urgency of Banaz's situation and moved her to a women's refuge immediately. She had just heard a young woman talk about repeatedly being raped, beaten and threatened with murder. Yet the police officer didn't seem to understand the severity of the situation.

'You've given us lines of inquiry that we'll need to follow up,' the officer responded, in a matter-of-fact tone. 'We'll let you know what's happening.' I would discover that it took them three months to simply write up her statement, while a police inquiry would later find that they made no effort to trace her husband or investigate further. This was just the first of many failures in the handling of Banaz's case.

In December that same year, Banaz overheard her uncle Ari on the phone to her mother, talking of how Banaz and her boyfriend had to die. 'They are bringing shame on the family and that bitch and that bastard are going to die,' he said.

Banaz hand-delivered a letter to the police providing details of the plot to kill her including the names of men who 'were ready and willing to do the job of killing me and my boyfriend'. This was one of five encounters she had with police over a five-month period in which every opportunity to save her was lost.

On New Year's Eve, the family decided it was time. Her father tricked Banaz into going to her grandmother's house, then forced her to gulp down brandy. She had never consumed alcohol before and the effects left her reeling. The curtains were drawn and cartoons were playing on the television. Leaving the room, Banaz's father told her to sit back on the sofa because she would soon feel sleepy. When he returned, he told her to watch the television and not turn around – but she did, and so saw him approaching wearing surgical gloves. She knew immediately that he was going to try to kill her. He went to grab her by the neck, but she managed to break free from his clutches and push him away before bolting out of the house. Utterly terrified, she screamed and plunged her hands through the neighbour's back window in a desperate attempt to attract attention. Her arms and wrists now bleeding heavily, she somehow managed to scale the back fence and run barefoot down the street, shouting for help. She collapsed on the floor of a nearby café and was taken to hospital in an ambulance, telling the crew that her father and uncle had tried to kill her. Then she called Rahmat to warn him.

The police were called and, when Rahmat arrived at the

hospital, he took out his mobile phone and asked Banaz to explain what had happened, recording her answer as evidence. He didn't think people would believe what her family had done. The shaky mobile footage of Banaz lying on a hospital bed, explaining how she had narrowly escaped being killed by her father, is shocking. A member of hospital staff who looked after her that night said that they had never seen anyone so frightened in their life. Indeed, staff had to fetch a security guard to assure Banaz it was safe enough to leave the ambulance, so scared was she for her life. But, shamefully, the police officer who was sent to the hospital didn't believe her: it was considered that she was just a girl who had drank too much and was worried that she was going to be in trouble. The officer even considered charging her for the criminal damage she had caused to her neighbour's window. It was astonishing and heartbreaking.

Banaz knew she was incredibly lucky to be alive. But her family weren't going to make the same mistake twice. Not long afterwards, she sent what was to be her final text message to Rahmat.

I love you so much xxx

Then she disappeared.

Of course, Rahmat knew something terrible had happened when he couldn't reach Banaz. He went straight to the police and reported her missing. Finally, the police were to be confronted with the result of their errors. Banaz's family insisted she hadn't gone missing and had simply gone to stay with a friend, but Detective Inspector Caroline Goode, who was leading the investigation, knew something wasn't right. Not only was there Rahmat's evidence and Banaz's own testimony, but no one in the Kurdish community would talk to her. People either claimed to know nothing or told lies which were easily disproved. When DI Goode visited the family, she was struck by their lack of interest in their daughter's whereabouts. There were no pictures of Banaz in her parents' house. It was as if she had never existed.

DI Goode was now so sure that something had happened to Banaz that she opened a homicide investigation instead of a missing person's investigation, which would grant her greater resources to investigate the case. She began by looking into the five men that Banaz had told police were planning to kill her. Three were cousins and one of them, Mohamad Hama, had recently used a hire car with a GPS tracker. Following his movements over the period in which Banaz had disappeared, police saw that he had travelled to an address in Handsworth, just outside Birmingham city centre. There, tragically, they found Banaz. She was buried in a suitcase in the back garden of a terraced house, beneath a fridge. Curled up in a foetal position, she wore nothing but her knickers. Police would later find out she had suffered a brutal and agonisingly slow death on the morning of 24 January 2006.

Her father and mother had left the family home early,

leaving the coast clear for her killers. Banaz was asleep on the living-room floor, as she didn't have a room of her own. She was woken by Mohamad Ali, Mohamad Hama and Omar Hussein bursting into the room. Sickening details of her death would emerge after the police covertly recorded Hama in prison openly boasting of raping and beating Banaz, before strangling her to death. Hama told his cell-mate that he had raped her because he wanted her to know who was in control. This gruesome ordeal lasted for most of the morning.

'I swear to God it took more than two hours,' he said, laughing. 'Her soul and her life would not leave.' It was hard to feel anything other than revulsion, hearing these details when I later prepared the prosecution of the case.

Hama was facing a life sentence after pleading guilty to the crime. We also wanted to prosecute Banaz's father and uncle on circumstantial evidence. But Hama's two partners in crime, Mohamad Ali and Omar Hussein, had fled the country to Iraq. I wanted to do everything we could to get them back in the UK to face justice and was encouraged to see the police demanding the same.

I could see that DI Goode was ashamed at the police failings which had prevented Banaz from being saved. Once on the case she had led a remarkable investigation, driven by a single-minded determination to find Banaz and bring her killers to justice. She understood honour crime in a way that few other officers did and felt she had a duty to protect these young women. And like me, she was set on getting the other two perpetrators.

Soon afterwards, we began to get intelligence reports from Iraq that Mohamad and Omar were boasting openly about Banaz's murder. The idea of a goat or lamb being sacrificed for a celebratory feast, with people cheering and slapping the two 'heroes' on the back for restoring honour to the family, did not sit well with anyone. We knew Omar was being housed by his brother, who was a senior police officer in Iraq, and that many people there thought the pair of them had done nothing wrong. The two men felt they were untouchable.

Meanwhile, we faced other challenges. We had never extradited anyone from Iraq before. But in post-invasion Iraq the country was being run by a transitional government, so I was hopeful that we might make some headway, and I asked my CPS colleagues to explore every avenue to secure the return of Mohamad Ali and Omar Hussein to Britain. Initially the view of the extradition team at the CPS was that this was a bridge too far, particularly when we factored in an unstable government, but I told the CPS Head of Extradition that at the very least, we needed to try. We had to send out a clear message, I said, that we would not accept or tolerate this kind of behaviour. It would be a vital first step in changing the culture on a wider scale. Without taking these steps, I believed we would never stop honour killing. The team agreed, and we worked tirelessly to make it happen.

After much negotiation, we got a deal. In 2010, for the first time in history, two Iraqi citizens were extradited to face trial in the UK. I would have loved to have seen the look on the faces of Ali and Hussein when police appeared to arrest them and put them on a plane bound for London but, as it was, I was just delighted to have been part of the team who had made it possible. Both men were subsequently jailed for life.

We now had six men in jail and a seventh, who had helped bury Banaz's corpse, was also jailed for eight years in 2013.

These were things to celebrate, but the additional tragedy in this case was that Banaz's death had not been inevitable. We could and should have saved her. Even today I wonder what kind of woman she would have become. She deserved to be happy, to make a life of her own. But her awful death left a powerful legacy, and for the first time the subject of honour killing became part of the national conversation. Deeyah Khan's 2012 documentary, *Banaz: A Love Story*, had a phenomenal impact. Not only did it win an International Emmy and countless other accolades, it was shown as part of UK police-training programmes. The raw, heartbreaking footage of Banaz telling police what was going to happen to her was electrifying. It was a wake-up call Britain couldn't ignore.

As I told Steve Allen and Detective Chief Superintendent Gerry Campbell, who was leading the Met's response to tackling hate crime, we couldn't just rely on a few specialist officers. Every officer in every force needed to know how to approach these cases. We had to get 120,000 officers trained up – and fast. There was an appetite to do this and, before long, guidelines for the police had been updated with far more detail, and new officers training at Hendon Police College were learning about forced marriage and honour crime.

It wasn't just the police who had to get to grips with this deadly crime, however. So I began to tour the country, giving talks on what we'd learned from Banaz's case at numerous conferences and speaking to teachers, GPs and social workers in every major city. Before long, every government institution had national guidelines for tackling honour-based violence. They learned not just how to spot potential victims and where to refer them to for the right support, but also to ensure confidentiality was paramount. It is inappropriate to put sensitive material on accessible databases, as we had found to our cost in other cases when information got back to families. Everything had to be behind encrypted passwords. Above all, they learned what the consequences were if they did nothing.

None of this could diminish the monumental failings surrounding Banaz's death. An Independent Police Complaints Commission inquiry into the police treatment of Banaz was heavily critical of the way her case had been handled, concluding that there was 'a lack of awareness' of honour-based violence. This was putting it mildly and, if I was honest, there remained huge gaps in our knowledge, and further evidence of institutional failure.

Every week I saw more evidence of how the murderers were outsmarting us. I saw police scrimping on costs, using family members to act as interpreters when young women had complained of violent threats from their husband. As terrified women sat in police interview rooms warning in Urdu that their lives were in danger, family members would translate to the police, saying there had been a terrible mistake and that she just wanted to go home.

Another catastrophic failure I saw was the police arranging for a woman to be moved to a women's refuge – but booking a local taxi firm to take her there. On too many occasions, the taxi was a local Asian firm who knew the woman's family and would disobey the instructions to take her to a refuge, returning her instead to her abusers. I even learned of one case where the criminals were using their local MP to put pressure on the police to help them find their daughter. The daughter in question had fled an abusive relationship and was staying in a refuge. The MP, who knew nothing of the danger the daughter was in, contacted the police. In this instance, thankfully, the force in question recognised the danger and did not share details of her whereabouts. But it was a frightening example of what we were up against and of the work we still had to do.

During the prosecution of Banaz's family members for her murder, I began working on the case of a teenage bride who had been beaten to death by her husband. Sabia Rani came to Leeds from Pakistan in 2005 following an arranged marriage. She couldn't speak a word of English, was completely isolated with no family or friends, and had received constant beatings ever since she had arrived in the UK. A Home Office pathologist said her injuries were the worst he had seen, comparable to those of car-crash victims. She had fifteen broken ribs and bruising to 90 per cent of her body. It was another horrific case, another life cut short.

Once again, I suspected the family was complicit in her death. After further investigation, there were four particular relations I wanted to find a way of charging for failing to protect her while she was abused. In the first case of its kind in the UK, we used the Domestic Violence Crime and Victims Act 2004 to put them in the dock. This new legislation had previously been used to prosecute a parent for standing by while the other parent killed a child – and, with the law specifically referring to 'a child or vulnerable person', I knew we had a good chance of being able to persuade the judge and jury that this law should apply to Sabia too. We made the case and, thankfully, judge and jury agreed. Three of the family members were sent to jail, with another receiving a suspended sentence.

This, I felt, was a real sign of progress: we were using the law to make things happen. Within a few years we had gone from a position of total ignorance to one where the rest of the world wanted to learn from us. We were leading the way. I even had calls from the US State Department asking how we had started to achieve our objectives around honour-based violence. We were training real specialists in the field and had concrete guidelines to observe. We would eventually establish the first National Day of Remembrance on 14 July, the birth-day of Shafilea Ahmed, to make sure those murdered in the name of honour were never forgotten. Most importantly of all, we were making a difference and protecting young women.

Our work on these cases eventually led to a new law: Forced Marriage Protection Orders were introduced through the Forced Marriage (Civil Protection) Act in 2007. This legislation allows the court to make an order in an emergency, either to prevent a forced marriage or to protect a victim who was leaving one. Women who were at risk of rape, enforced pregnancy and honour-based violence finally had the law on their side. Hundreds of these orders are now issued every year, with one recipient being only five years old. I was thrilled at their success, but those kinds of stories were a sobering reminder of the scale of the problem. Nevertheless, the Forced Marriage legislation was so successful that a number of other orders, including both FGM and Domestic Violence Protection Orders, were modelled on them, and I knew that we were saving lives as a result. This kept me going. I would occasionally get messages from people telling me that they were now free from harm as a result. This mattered. It made it all worthwhile.

The final honour crime case that I led on as a prosecutor was the murder of twenty-eight-year-old mother of two Geeta Aulakh in 2009. It was an organised hit – and another reminder that we had some way to go if we were to defeat gender terrorism.

Geeta's marriage had been a loveless one for some time, her husband subjecting her to years of emotional abuse. When she asked for a divorce, he took it as such an affront to him and his culture that he decided she deserved to die. He began to plot her murder.

As Geeta made her way through a suburban part of West London after work one evening, on her way to pick up her eight- and ten-year-old sons from the childminder, two men emerged from the shadows. One of them, a Sikh teenager, was brandishing a 14-inch machete and launched into a vicious attack. As Geeta held up her hands to try and protect herself, he cut her right hand straight off. She died in hospital shortly afterwards with horrific injuries.

We gathered enough evidence from the husband's telephone records to discover that he had offered a £5,000 bounty for the killing. The husband was jailed for life and the two other men each received twenty-two-year sentences.

Geeta was yards away from reaching her young sons at the moment she was killed. Police officers would soon knock on the door of the childminder to inform her of what had happened so close to her home. She couldn't bring herself to look the two children in the eyes and tell them that their mother was dead. Like every other honour case I'd worked on, the pain didn't end with a brutal murder. It left behind a trail of devastation and unbearable heartbreak. It destroyed lives.

Ten years after Banaz was killed by her family, Rahmat was living alone in Dorset, still struggling to come to terms with her death.

'She was my present, my future, my hope,' he had said in an interview following Banaz's death. 'She was the best thing that ever happened to me. My life went away when Banaz died. There is no life.'

On 20 March 2016 he texted his neighbour asking for the police to pick up his dog. Then he tied a noose around his neck and hanged himself.

If I could have increased Banaz's killers' sentence, then I would have done it. Because they had killed him too.

Much to the annoyance of Banaz's family, her name has lived on, becoming synonymous with the struggle for freedom from honour-based violence and male repression. Although she was buried in an unmarked grave, the Iranian and Kurdish Women's Rights Organisation (IKWRO), led by a remarkable woman called Diana Nammi, arranged for a tombstone to be made honouring her memory.

On 26 June 2007, the sun shone brightly in a cloudless sky, the energetic trilling of blue tits filling the air as I joined dozens of people filing into Morden Assembly Hall. Detective Inspector Caroline Goode was there, along with women from IKWRO and victims and survivors who had given up their family to leave home, run away and escape honour-based violence. We had come together for a special remembrance service for Banaz, to reflect on her life and what she meant to us all.

Sunlight flooded through the windows and dust motes danced in the beams of the hall as some of the women started to sing in Kurdish. Others prayed silently. I felt a lump in my throat as I thought of Banaz. Among the welcoming faces in that room, there was an immense feeling of togetherness. It was one of the most moving events I had ever attended, and I felt privileged even just to witness it. No one from Banaz's family attended. We were her family now.

Afterwards, we went to Merton and Sutton cemetery and placed the tombstone on Banaz's grave before saying prayers. My eyes lingered on the bold, gold lettering of her name on black granite. Banaz Mahmod would not be forgotten.

VII

In popular culture everyone loves the drama of the courtroom. And more often than not, it's the fearless defence lawyer who plays the hero. Prosecutors play second fiddle. Think of the bravura performances of Gregory Peck as Atticus Finch, Tom Cruise as Lieutenant Kaffee and Emma Thompson as Gareth Peirce. The contrast to the depiction of the prosecutor is often stark. We're led to believe that it's the crusading defence lawyer who chases down the truth to protect the innocent, while the arrogant prosecutor is a cruel manifestation of state power. Of course, there are exceptions. But, for the most part, prosecutors have never been associated with campaigning zeal.

Furthermore, there is a long history of the prosecutor being cast as an enemy who must be defeated. The figure of the prosecutor can be found as far back as the Old Testament. In Judaism, Satan is not seen as a fallen angel, but instead as a prosecutor appointed by God in the Book of Job to search an individual's wrongdoings and test the loyalty of Yahweh's followers. In Dostoevsky's *The Brothers Karamazov*, the prosecutor, Ippolit Kirillovich, is a narrow-minded, mediocre individual with a vengeful desire to condemn. And in John Grisham's novel *A Time to Kill*, the prosecutor is a racist so corrupt that he rigs the jury. Throughout literature, prosecutors are depicted as antagonists. We embody power without understanding, we're the law without a human face. Obviously, I don't share this view. On the contrary: I believe the prosecutor is a real agent of change for good.

I had always considered an important part of my job to be pioneering prosecutions in areas where there was yet to be legislation, such as honour-based violence. In truth, there were also more well-established laws that were failing the vulnerable and allowing perpetrators to evade justice. I wasn't just looking for new crimes to prosecute: I was looking to use our cases to *refine* the law, to bring it into line with the realities of modern Britain. One of the areas in which the law was often failing was domestic violence, and the case of Gurda Dhaliwal was a clear example of why the law needed to change.

Gurda was a forty-five-year-old mother of two when she walked into a shed in Southall, West London, in February 2005 with a rope. After twenty-five years of abuse from her husband, she'd had enough. Her youngest son would later discover her hanging there after he'd followed her footprints in the snow.

At first, there seemed to be no suspicious circumstances surrounding her death. Her husband said he was distraught and simply couldn't understand why his wife had chosen to end her life this way. It seemed a terrible tragedy, of course, but not one that required further investigation. A coroner went on to record a verdict of suicide and the case would normally have ended there.

But there was something about the case that didn't seem right. It first came to my attention after a prosecutor in my team flagged up the fact that, when Gurda was found hanged, she had a fresh cut to her forehead that was unlikely to have been self-inflicted. This made us pause: might there be something else at play here?

Hounslow police were interested in the cut too, and they brought in Gurda's husband for questioning. When they asked if there was anything we could do about the cut from a legal perspective, we told them a charge of common assault might be appropriate against her husband if we could prove that the wound was not accidental, and that it had been inflicted by him. When the police carried out a search of Gurda's home, they found her diary. I was instantly interested. My colleague Nikki, who had been the one to spot Gurda's injury, brought me a copy of it the very next day. I held it in my hand, hesitant to open it and discover what was inside. And then I started to read Gurda's thoughts on her final days.

'It's a handwritten record of domestic abuse,' Nikki said. 'Most of it is non-violent, but it's domestic abuse nonetheless.'

Those pages documented the last five months of her life and as I traced the nervous, spidery handwriting, I imagined the anguish in Gurda's heart as she surreptitiously scribbled details of the harrowing day-to-day torment she endured. Each entry would no doubt have been hurriedly recorded, as she must have known she was risking serious punishment if her husband caught her in the act or ever found the diary.

It documented cruel psychological abuse – a callous and controlling pattern of behaviour that would be all too familiar to the thousands of people suffering in silence every year in the UK. At first, Gurda and her husband had been like any newly married couple; happy and in love. But reading the diary we learned that her husband became increasingly abusive and controlling over the years. Gurda temporarily left her husband on a number of occasions, yet each time she returned and, each time, the abuse got worse.

He began to limit who she could see and when she could go out. Then he began to control what she wore, when she went to work and even when she could see her family. Eventually, he cut her off completely from everyone. He kept her in a prison of her own isolation.

At the time, the law didn't adequately deal with the kind of abuse that Gurda was suffering, and it would take another decade before it began to address such behaviour formally. At that time, abuse had to be violence of a physical nature in order to be criminal. We had the cut on her forehead, but did a common assault charge with a maximum six-month imprisonment penalty truly recognise the impact of the behaviour recorded in Gurda's diary? I didn't think so. This, I thought, would be an opportunity to explore what we could do with the law.

Pushing the boundaries was particularly challenging in the case of domestic abuse, because it was often so difficult for victims to come forward. Research by the British Medical Association shows that victims might experience an average of thirty-five incidents before taking action. That's a lot of abuse and some victims will experience many more instances. It is also the case that minorities often struggled the most in this way. A charity supporting people with disabilities told me that on average, victims with disabilities suffered twice as many abusive incidents before reporting, compared to able-bodied victims. If you are reliant upon someone to be your carer, then it may be that in your mind you are balancing every day whether the abuse you're getting is 'your fault', and the opportunities to raise the alarm are often more infrequent. In my research, I also spoke to victims of LGBTQI+ domestic abuse and found that perceived discrimination around same-sex relationships was also a barrier to seeking help.

I made another call to Southall Black Sisters in West London, and that was even more illuminating. They had further research showing that South Asian women were three times less likely to report abuse because of issues related to honour and shame. If you were someone like Gurda, then, you might endure an average of a hundred incidents of abuse before you had the courage to tell anyone about it. Having read her diary, I felt certain that Gurda had been driven to suicide by her husband's abusive and controlling behaviour. How many other women were in the same position, I wondered. And could I find a way of prosecuting Gurda's husband for causing her to take her life?

The offence of manslaughter occurs when a person does something, or omits to do something, that leads to another person's death. It carries a maximum life imprisonment. If a medical practitioner gave an accidental overdose, that gross negligence could be manslaughter. If a person opened a door that led to a child falling to their death, that might also be manslaughter. The connection in these instances is negligence.

Another form of manslaughter involves an 'unlawful act' leading to another's death. Imagine, for example, if a person was pushed away by another, and as a result, lost their footing and fell to their death. There may not be an intention to kill here, or even to hurt another person, but nevertheless these actions lead to someone's death. The important point is 'causation'.

In Gurda's case I could argue that her husband's psychological abuse of her was unlawful and that ultimately, it caused her death. However, Gurda took her own life, and this added a level of complexity to proceedings. We had photos of injuries she had shown her family over the months: bruises, cuts, a black eye. We had statements from her family that she had disclosed beatings, threats and general hostility allegedly at the hands of her husband. Then there was her diary. I could see from her own writing that she had suffered so much abuse it had led her to contemplate suicide. In my mind, that meant the abuse was either 'grossly negligent' or at the very least, a series of 'unlawful acts'. I felt we were on reasonable territory but at the end of the day, my own reasoning was untested. I needed soundings from others, so I instructed counsel to advise me on whether I had a basis in law to bring a prosecution for manslaughter. I also instructed three experts in psychological harm to advise me on whether, and how, the law protected Gurda.

It seems an obvious thing to say, but much of the law is decades, even centuries, old and therefore not necessarily fit for purpose in Britain today. In this instance, we were relying on Victorian legislation that was passed even before psychiatry in its modern sense existed. The Offences Against the Persons Act of 1861 is the British legal foundation for prosecuting personal injury short of murder. But it was very much of its time: the crimes listed in the Act included one of impeding a person endeavouring to save himself from shipwreck, and another of causing assault with the intention of preventing the sale of grain or its free passage. It was a relic from another age and did nothing to address injuries such as emotional abuse. And in 2005 we were still years from the Serious Crime Act of 2015, which made behaviour that is 'coercive or controlling' towards another person in an intimate or family relationship punishable by a prison term of up to five years.

Nevertheless, while legislation hadn't yet caught up with

our contemporary understanding of crime, we were starting to widen our understanding of violence, trying to think about the role of 'psychological injury' and how we might interpret that in court. The law requires 'bodily harm', but research in medicine had showed that psychiatric harm *is* also bodily harm, because it involves damage to the nervous system, and stress and psychological illness can manifest themselves in physical ways. Legal ruling in this area was certainly rather incoherent but we felt that if we could prove that Gurda's husband had inflicted such harm on her that it had led to her taking her own life, then he could potentially be held liable for her death. It was something of a gamble, but the thought of Gurda's children spurred me on.

By now I had also met with Gurda's extraordinary brother Nav Jagpal. Consumed by grief, he was determined to get justice for his sister. Refuge, the national charity for domestic violence victims, was supporting and advising him. In meetings with Nav and the head of Refuge, Sandra Horley, I was continuing to learn more about the scale of the problem. Alongside the remarkable work Refuge do, they also gather research: they had discovered that thirty women a day attempt suicide as a result of experiencing domestic abuse in the UK, and every week three women take their own lives to escape abuse.

If I looked at Gurda's case on a code test basis, ensuring I was satisfied there was enough evidence to provide a 'realistic prospect of conviction', then there was a high chance it would fail – and I had to be honest about the fact that this outcome was a strong probability. Partly, this was because it was going to be extremely difficult to prove that Gurda had a recognisable psychiatric condition at the time of her death. However, I had a plan.

There was a reasonable chance that the Old Bailey would throw out our case. This, however, would then allow me to take it to the Court of Appeal and so give us an opportunity to examine the law thoroughly and push for meaningful change. I was confident that from there, I could get the Court of Appeal to agree that you can be guilty of driving someone to suicide.

Several of my colleagues questioned my thinking, and I could see why: what is the point of bringing a case if it is going to fail? However, I was thinking beyond just this one case. If it failed, then it would be because the law wasn't clear enough. And that had to change. But how?

When Parliament decides to pass legislation, it is a long, complex process dependent on there being a consensus among MPs to deliver change. There is an alternative to this, however: to have the law 'clarified' through judicial interpretation. The Supreme Court doesn't actually change the law; it instead clarifies how it should be applied to something never addressed before. This can drive significant developments.

By seeking to clarify the law in relation to Gurda's case, I was aiming for momentous change. Parliament wasn't a realistic option given the timescale involved, but if I pursued the case in the courts and the Crown Court declined to take it forward because of their interpretation of the law, then I could go to the Court of Appeal. That's where we could scrutinise the law properly, to get the clarity that I felt was so desperately needed. I wanted to show that in some circumstances, with the right evidence, someone could be guilty of manslaughter if they drove someone to suicide.

Indeed, for me it was a win – win situation. If the Crown Court agreed with this manslaughter proposition, I would get justice for Gurda. If the judge said the law wasn't clear enough for the case to be prosecuted, I had the option of going to the Court of Appeal. If I got a result there, all the lower courts would have to abide by its adjudication. This would go on to ensure that similar cases would result in a trial, with people being prosecuted for driving others to suicide.

Meanwhile, Gurda's husband had finally admitted to hitting her on the evening she died, so we could get him on a common assault charge if we wished. We had a much bigger result in our grasp now and I advised my team and counsel that we would proceed on a manslaughter charge. It was a landmark test case and the NGOs working with domestic abuse expressed their delight at the risk I was taking. 'We're going to give it our best shot,' was my frequent response whenever I was asked about its chances of success.

Some of my colleagues felt that this was simply too much of a departure from our code, and that changes to the law must pass through Parliament. But I wasn't seeking to undermine any of these processes: Gurda's case had really got to me, and I simply wanted to seize this opportunity to bring her justice. Still, it didn't make me a popular man at the CPS, and I was starting to find that when I wanted to meet with a charity, I would be told that middle management wanted to sit in.

'You cannot be seen to be campaigning for a change in the law,' they would maintain. 'We suggest changes to legislation quietly, in briefing documents.' It was our job to *apply* the law, not change it.

'I'm simply trying to clarify the law,' was my response. If we couldn't clarify it, then we couldn't apply it.

The truth was that of course I wanted to see change, because then the law could do a better job of protecting vulnerable people. At times it was our job to facilitate change, at times it was necessary – as with, for example, the issue of forced marriage.

In court, we had to show that what Gurda had suffered was not just psychological harm, but also *psychiatric* harm. We'd need to make the case that she had suffered from a recognised condition, such as post-traumatic stress syndrome, and that this had amounted to bodily harm, which in turn had led to manslaughter.

We had always known this would be difficult, not least because normally a psychiatrist would provide a report based on an interview with a living person. But we obviously couldn't do this, so I had to ask experts to review evidence collected by the police and from witness statements in order to form a view of the mental health of someone who was no longer with us.

Expert evidence is vital in court: there are times where no jury member could be expected to make a decision without it, when an expert is essential for relaying and explaining what can be deduced from the evidence. Experts give their evidence and are cross-examined by barristers, before the judge and jury then decide which account is most credible.

For the prosecution team, this can create problems. If a prosecutor instructs – brings to court – an expert, and that expert contradicts one of the others the prosecution has relied on, then we are required by law to disclose that report to the defence because it may undermine our case or assist theirs. The law is absolutely clear here. The police and prosecution must disclose their case in its entirety to the defence, where it's relevant and admissible. This includes even evidence that we don't rely upon, evidence that potentially contradicts evidence we are submitting. We do this because of the established legal standard that the prosecution must prove beyond reasonable doubt.

That same rule, however, does not apply to the defence team. They can ask several experts for their views and only divulge the ones they are choosing to use in court. It's simple, in our legal system; the prosecution needs to prove the case, the defence doesn't have to prove a thing.

We worked hard to find the right experts, and in the end I brought three of them to court. They went through all the material we had collected and two out of the three agreed that, yes, it was likely that Gurda suffered PTSD. The third couldn't be sure. The defence, of course, brought to the stand their own expert, who came to the conclusion that no psychiatric harm could be proved.

We went before Judge Roberts QC at the Old Bailey, knowing that the defence had not only our two experts' reports proving our case, but also the one that was non-committal. Yet although this third report undeniably created a modicum of doubt, which was potentially problematic for us, we were still confident that our argument was strong.

And so we presented our case, giving a summary of the evidence and expert testimony as well as statements from Gurda's family, to take us to the stage at which the judge would then decide whether there was a case to answer, requiring legal representations from both sides to assist him. If the decision was in our favour, then we would proceed to trial.

The result, when it came, was a crushing disappointment. The judge threw out charges of manslaughter and grievous bodily harm because there was no basis on which a jury could convict Gurda's husband. While he acknowledged Gurda had suffered psychological injury, the judge could not determine 'psychiatric injury' and therefore we didn't meet the definition of bodily harm required by the law. The judge did acknowledge that the law was unclear but this, he said, was the very reason that the defendant could not be convicted of breaking it. I understood his perspective, but heartily disagreed with the outcome. Now, we were heading to the Court of Appeal.

A few months later, we returned to put our case before Sir Igor Judge, Mr Justice Henriques and Mr Justice Fulford. As I told them, I wanted the court to consider whether there were any circumstances in which someone can ever be found guilty of driving another person to suicide. They agreed in principle but frustratingly, also upheld the previous decision that the case could not proceed, as they did not believe Gurda's case crossed the evidential threshold. Sir Igor did, however, call for a review of the law and established the principle that, with the appropriate medical evidence, it is possible to prosecute someone for driving another person to suicide.

'It is very hard not to see some connection between the incident of violence which appears to have taken place shortly before, and her death,' said the judge, in summing up. At last, we had the breakthrough I wanted. In recognising that cruel and controlling behaviour which causes a recognised psychiatric illness could trigger someone to take their life, we made sure this crime would come under the scope of manslaughter in future judgments.

'I would have thought there was some force in the argument that the "last straw" played a significant part in causing her death,' concluded the judge. We might not have had the conviction we wanted but that night I took stock of our successes nonetheless.

Soon after, I wrote to the Coroners' Society of England and Wales and sent the senior coroner, André Rebello, a copy of the Court of Appeal's judgment. In my letter, I acknowledged we did not have enough evidence but argued that the police will never gather enough evidence to make prosecutions unless coroners refer cases to the police for further investigation. They would do this in an unlawful killing, but in a suicide scenario I had never heard of such a referral.

Rebello wrote back saying he would like to discuss this further. When we met, he accepted that he and his fellow coroners were gatekeepers to cases being potentially investigated by the police and their guidelines needed to be refreshed in line with this judgment. He agreed to issue instructions to all coroners that if such a situation occurred again, they should adjourn the inquest and notify the police to investigate possible manslaughter based on driven suicide. Finally, we were creating the framework to re-evaluate these crimes, and ensure the conviction of those guilty. People would eventually be arrested, charged and convicted for manslaughter when their partners had killed themselves as a direct result of domestic abuse and controlling behaviour.

Making our courts fit for purpose in the twenty-first century was no easy task. We were patiently chiselling away at the crusty patina of antiquity that was on show in our courts every week. I remembered the case of a High Court judge in an internet terrorism trial, who famously said he didn't understand what a website was.

It wasn't just laws from 150 years ago that were making it impossible for the justice system to keep up with modern crimes. Society changes so fast that even laws that are just a few decades old can quickly become outdated. The Public Order Act of 1986 was one example of this. When the Danish newspaper *Jyllands-Posten* published a series of cartoons in 2005, depicting the Prophet Mohammed, it would spark a wave of protests that would challenge the way we dealt with demonstrations.

Muslims reject images of all prophets, including Jesus, Moses, Abraham and Mohammed. They take very literally the commandment issued to Moses that 'thou shall not bow down before any graven image', in the belief that to do so makes an Idol of that image, and therefore equates that person with God.

The Danish images were considered highly blasphemous, including one with the Prophet Mohammed wearing a bomb in his turban. When a Norwegian newspaper reprinted them, protests began to spread across the Middle East. And they didn't stop there. When newspapers in France, Germany, Italy and Spain chose to reprint the caricatures the protests spread like wildfire through those countries too. Finally, they reached the UK.

In February 2006, hundreds of members of the extreme Islamist groups al Ghurabaa and the Saviour Sect gathered outside the London Central Mosque after Friday prayers and marched to the Danish embassy. As the first loudhailer crackled into life, it was immediately obvious this was not going to be a peaceful protest. Clenched fists punched the air and shouts of 'Jihad in the name of Allah!' rose above the angry cacophony of demonstrators. There were calls for British troops to return home in body bags and chants of 'Bomb, bomb the UK.' The air vibrated with violence as more threats boomed from loudhailers.

'You have declared war against Allah and his prophet,' screamed one protestor, 'for which you will pay a heavy price.'

Another voice called out the name of Theo van Gogh, the outspoken Dutch film director who had been critical of Islam and was shot and stabbed to death on an Amsterdam street. Amidst the chanting and speeches, a sea of placards and make-shift cardboard signs bore such slogans as 'Behead the one who insults the prophet', 'Massacre those who insult Islam' and 'Be prepared for the real Holocaust'. It was a frightening scene and came only a few months after a series of Islamist ter-rorist suicide attacks had devastated London. I watched aghast, despairing at how some British Muslims were using the admit-tedly provocative cartoons to feed a political and ideological agenda. It played right into the hands of Islamophobes and, more than that, these demonstrations often provoked vio-lence: across the globe, people had been killed in them.

I have always believed in the importance of free speech, but when the expression of that free speech threatens others, the law needs to intervene. I also took the view that my own faith is not weakened by somebody taking the piss and if it was, then it would hardly be faith at all. The problem with freedoms is that they often create tension with others, and as a result the business of deciding which freedom takes priority is in constant flux. We've seen this tension more recently in Birmingham schools where the right to teach children about homosexuality appears to conflict with the right of those families who believe that, according to their scriptures, being gay is a sin. Everyone has their own beliefs and adjudicating between them is a constant challenge. In these situations, the law of the land has to step in to determine the limits of any freedom. That's where the 'hate laws', such as racially and religiously aggravated public order, usually come into play. These were passed by Blair's Labour government in 1998 under the Crime and Disorder Act. The aim was to stamp out discrimination and abuse, and it directed the courts to enhance sentences where offences were aggravated by racism or religious hatred.

But sometimes these laws are not enough.

In this case I felt a minor public order charge, which usually applied where demonstrations of this kind were concerned, would not address the severity of the situation. These protestors were deliberately stirring up hatred, urging violent acts that may well result in people being killed. After the aggressors were taken into custody, I met with the public order prosecutors to look at the evidence against all the protesters who had been arrested, including evidence provided by the police of previous criminal activity. This clarified things in my mind. I went to see the Director of Public Prosecutions, Ken Macdonald, to put forward my view that we had enough evidence to charge these people with soliciting murder. To my delight, he agreed with my assessment and, accordingly, the case was transferred to the Counter Terrorism Unit. As a result of their part in the protests, four men came to be jailed for six years each for soliciting murder.

This was an important moment for me, because it signified how we could become more effective at protecting the public if we were able to think laterally and apply our laws with a certain flexibility of thought. We didn't normally charge people with soliciting murder for this type of behaviour and that was because, as the judge told the jury in the trial, 'freedoms of speech and assembly have long been jealously guarded by our laws'. But those freedoms carried responsibility – and the protesters had crossed a line into dangerous territory. We faced protests from both human rights lawyers and extreme Islamist groups, but I felt confident that the streets were safer as a result.

A few weeks later, however, I would discover the personal toll that my work could have. Finishing off my emails after a day at my desk, there was a knock on my office door.

'Nazir, there's someone from Special Branch to see you,' a colleague announced.

'OK,' I replied, feeling puzzled. 'Send them in.'

The officer strode purposefully into my office and took a seat, before informing me that my name had appeared as a potential target on a verified al-Qaeda hit list.

'It's presumably because of your public announcements on the Danish cartoon case,' he added.

I struggled to take it in. I asked him exactly what it meant. 'And what are you going to do about it?' I added.

'I've just done it,' he said. 'My job is to inform you of the threat and we'll update you as and when.'

'Update?' I queried. 'Is that likely to happen before they carry out their threat?'

'Hopefully,' he replied.

I went home that night and hugged my kids a little more tightly. But I wasn't planning to change anything.

VIII

It was late when I slipped the key in the lock of my front door. I turned it gently, so I didn't disturb my family as they slept. It was always late these days. Everyone was in bed and the house was quiet. I scanned the post on the kitchen table, put the kettle on and picked up the school photos of our children that my wife had left out. The kettle whirred to its whistle as I fondly traced my finger around their smiling faces, thinking of all the things I was missing out on in their lives. The school plays, concerts, birthday parties, sports days. They were growing up fast and there was so much I wanted to know, but never had the time to ask them. What excited them? What friends were they making? Which teachers did they like? I was an absent father in my own home. It was so easy to become absorbed by my work and the community engagement. I couldn't remember the last time we had taken a holiday. Life in London, which had once seemed so fresh and exciting, now seemed exhausting. Maybe I wasn't just a stranger to my kids. I felt as though I was becoming a stranger to myself.

And while the work was always rewarding, lately I was feeling the weight of it on my shoulders. The threats from al-Qaeda had, thank God, come to nothing, but I had realised that my work was making me more of a public figure than I had ever expected. And it wasn't just the religious extremists. Increasingly, as so much of my work involved finding ways into communities with cultural differences, I found myself coming into contact with groups from the resurgent far right, who had been watching my cases with interest. As I took an interest in honour crime, which was more prevalent in Asian communities, they thought they could weaponise me, use my work as a way of realising their racist agendas, 'proving' that immigrant communities were dangerous. It was exhausting stuff. But then, I was used to the race card being played.

By now, we were living in a time of coalition government and in the autumn of 2010 I was invited to join David Cameron for the launch of a national wellbeing project. I have to be honest, the call was a bit of a surprise: this wasn't really my area. As I went to take my seat at the back of the room, I got a tap on the shoulder from an adviser.

'Nazir, would you kindly come this way?'

I was ushered to the front of the room, where I was seated in front of the podium before the Prime Minister. I was somewhat bemused: this campaign had nothing to do with me. It dawned on me: I looked around at the 200 civil servants present and could see immediately that they had a diversity problem. As Cameron made his way to the front, the cameras homed in on me. I was, I presumed, there to give the impression it was a diverse audience when, in fact, I was the only person of colour in the room. It struck me what a waste of time this all was, when I could be at home with my kids. My mind drifted away from the speech happening at the front of the room as I thought about this, imagining the children getting ready for bed, curled up under the covers.

Cameron was now moving on to the central part of his argument; that the serious business of government was to make life better for people and that we needed a national debate about what really matters. Perhaps we did. But for me, this all suddenly felt very personal. I had to work out for myself what mattered.

Meanwhile, I knew that changes were on the horizon at work. The CPS had to regionalise because of cuts to their budget and I heard that as a result, there would be opportunities to work as a regional prosecutor. There were forty-three Chief Prosecutors in the regions at that time, but in the new order there would be fourteen. This made each role a little more powerful, and therefore a little more enticing. Plus, lately I'd been thinking about getting out of London. Maybe not Birmingham: I wanted a totally fresh start. I began to think about Manchester. I didn't know anyone in the north of England, didn't really have any connections there, but it could be the opportunity I had been looking for to put some distance between myself and London. My family, to my surprise, loved the idea, even if it meant relocating, and after some conversations with my bosses, it was decided that in four months I would make the move and take up the North West Chief Crown Prosecutor job. What I didn't know then was that my move to Manchester, far from giving me a less pressurised job, would be the start of the most challenging period of my career. But in the meantime, I comforted myself with the knowledge that the drive to work from my new home would only take thirty minutes, so I would be able to spend more time with my children and wife, enjoying the more family-friendly working practices in the Manchester office. The retention rate was much higher than in London. People stayed there for a long time. All of this was music to my ears.

While I worked out my notice, I took some time to look at the strategic issues facing the region, and to try and get a sense of the work that needed doing there. And that's when I came across Andrew Norfolk's investigations in *The Times*.

Norfolk was the newspaper's chief investigative reporter and he was based in Leeds. At that time, he was investigating child sexual exploitation cases up and down the country and had written a series of incendiary pieces on how gangs of mainly Pakistani men were grooming underage white girls for sex. He exposed an appalling scandal in Rotherham and was starting to make deeply disturbing connections with similar patterns of abuse everywhere. The stories were horrifying, and I suspected that in my new job, I might be able to get involved in investigating some of these crimes.

The far right, and most notably the British National Party (BNP), were capitalising on Norfolk's articles and starting to make some predictably racist political noise about the issue. This was evident from their online forums and newsletters, and, in the same spirit of reaching out and listening to people that had guided me throughout my career, I decided to get in touch with them to ask what they wanted the law to do differently. I made contact with the BNP to ask them what their concerns were, and I think it's fair to say that they were surprised when I told them I wanted to talk about Asian grooming gangs.

'Hello,' I said. 'It's Nazir Afzal here from the Crown Prosecution Service.' It was clear that they hadn't expected me to follow through on the promise I'd made in an email, that I would give them a call to hear them out.

'I see you're complaining about the fact we're not prosecuting grooming cases with any vigour,' I said, 'so I want to get your views on how you think we should improve our work.'

'What do you mean?'

'Well, do you think we should produce more expert evidence, for example, to make sure the jury understands what is happening to these girls?'

It became pretty obvious that they didn't really have much of a clue. We argued first about the challenges of these prosecutions: the question of consent being such a thorny issue, given that there was often a degree of ignorance in the courtroom which meant that these girls, often children who might have had problems in their families or in their education, were said to be knowing what they were getting themselves into. So, I asked them, what were their ideas on dealing with that? There was silence, until the voice at the end of the phone piped up that all we needed to focus on was the ethnicity of the perpetrators. It was only ever one thing with them, and I seriously doubted whether they cared about the welfare of these girls at all: for them, it was just a way of making their usual warped point.

Still, I thought, it always good to have a chat. I asked the voice on the line if people at the BNP might like to meet with me to discuss the issue further.

'No. I'm sorry, but they wouldn't want to meet with you.'

'Is that because I'm a prosecutor?'

'No, it's because of who you are.'

This was becoming a common theme. Often those that made the loudest noise about crime usually had no interest in finding solutions to protecting those most at risk or delivering justice. Stephen Yaxley-Lennon, otherwise known as Tommy Robinson, was another example. I believed he had no real interest in any of the victims he claimed to care about. He was after a religious war and would use anything or anyone to stoke those flames.

Nevertheless, I could see that what Norfolk had unearthed was a national problem. And as I drove up the M6 in May 2011 to start our new life in Manchester, I suspected I would soon be devoting a lot of time and energy to dealing with it.

*

I had been a little apprehensive about the move, but I need not have worried. I settled into Manchester straight away and soon became familiar with the regional skyline, travelling the M56, M62, M6 and M61 between our offices. The giant wind turbines, rugged high fells and the shifting colours of vast northern skies were the perfect antidote to the claustrophobia I often felt in London. And I was relieved that the family felt the same. In fact, my youngest son, a Manchester United fan, was positively ecstatic. It was, he said, like he'd finally come home. Soon after, I took him to Old Trafford to watch his first game where, incredibly, Manchester United beat Arsenal 8 – 2. What a welcome.

The first thing I noticed when I arrived at my new office on Quay Street was that staff morale was extremely good. It was a tight knit-team, with lot of experienced staff who immediately made me feel welcome. My office was next to the complex casework unit and I would be working closely with two highly experienced lawyers, Fran Gough and John Dilworth, who would both prove to be invaluable. I felt that I would be able to do some good work in Manchester.

Still, there were a few mysteries to solve. In the corner of my room was a large, dusty safe.

'What's in there?' I asked John.

'I don't know,' he said. 'No one's ever opened it.'

I couldn't find a key, so for a while the safe simply sat in the corner, continuing to gather dust. A year later, when I was trying to find police files on the late Liberal MP, Sir Cyril Smith,

I decided we had to open it. Smith had died in 2010 and allegations that he had been a serial child abuser were now coming to the fore in much the same way as they had about Jimmy Savile. Maybe the files I was looking for were inside. Lancashire Constabulary had admitted they'd lost the password to access the Smith files online, so I was running out of ideas. Perhaps, I said, I could get a locksmith in and bust it open.

And indeed, when the locksmith finally wrenched the door open, Smith's files were hidden inside. Along with Dr Harold Shipman's medical bag. Manchester was proving to be full of surprises.

But back in that first week, I brought up the child sexual exploitation cases that Andrew Norfolk was reporting on. Did the team know of any cases like this on our books?

'Yes,' said Fran immediately. 'We've got one case in particular and it's a serious problem.'

She brought me up to speed on Operation Span, an investigation that had been launched by Greater Manchester Police following complaints from forty-seven girls that they had been raped by grooming gangs in Rochdale. Fran explained that these cases followed exactly the same pattern of abuse of young white girls by British Asian men that Norfolk had been writing about. However, she said, the police had known about the complaints for some time and a decision had been taken in 2009 by the CPS not to prosecute on the grounds that the victims were 'not credible'. The problem hadn't gone away, though. More girls were coming forward with similar complaints and the police were looking at the possibility of reopening the case. I took a look through the case history and as I scanned the documents, I could see that old cliché – a catalogue of errors.

'This investigation doesn't look great,' I told Fran. 'They spent eleven months investigating one of the victims instead of the suspects. What's that about?'

The look on Fran's face told me she felt the same. She told me that she had the original interviews on DVD, if I wanted to watch them. Absolutely, I said.

That evening I watched the footage of a fifteen-year-old girl being interviewed by police back in 2008. She was the teenager the CPS had labelled 'not credible' and would later become known as 'Girl A'. The look on her face as she spoke of being raped repeatedly by a gang of men was heart-rending, but the thing that really stood out to me was an officer's indifference. At one point he even yawned while the girl was sharing excruciatingly painful, intimate information. It was hard to watch, but I was on the edge of my seat. Immediately I knew that this was a case we needed to take up.

We were over six years away from the breakthrough of #MeToo. But the seismic cultural shift and empowerment that this movement began didn't start in Hollywood. And it didn't even begin with Alyssa Milano's tweet urging people who had been sexually harassed or assaulted to start a conversation using the #MeToo hashtag. It started even further back.

The seeds for the most powerful movement in a generation had been sown on a global scale years before. The fightback against abuse of power, victim blaming and everyday harassment was happening in refuges, safe-space workshops and specialist sexual health services everywhere.

In 2017, *Time* magazine announced that its person of the year was the 'silence breakers'; the women and men who had come forward to shed light on sexual harassment and abuse. But as I sat watching Girl A's interview that night in 2011, I knew I was witnessing something significant, a moment in which the silence around this vile abuse was being broken. It was thanks to the bravery, determination and resilience of ordinary young girls in towns across the country. These were girls whose voices had never been heard before. They didn't have expensive lawyers, social standing or well-connected people to advocate for them. To the authorities, they didn't count. One police officer even described these girls as 'scrubbers'. To society, they may as well have been invisible.

The next day I called a meeting to discuss the case.

'Did you watch the DVD?' Fran asked. I nodded. 'And?'

'I think she's telling the truth. I believe her.'

Fran's face lit up.

'So do I,' she agreed, smiling.

The whole team was in agreement. We would have to put things right.

IX

The car door flung open and two girls were pushed out into the darkness. They fell awkwardly onto the moorland heather, as the car accelerated away and the taillights disappeared into the night. The girls grabbed each other, huddling together, frozen in fear. After several minutes, when they were sure the car wasn't coming back, they looked across the barren land-scape of Saddleworth Moors towards the lights of civilisation blinking faintly in the distance. Then they began the long fourteen-mile walk back to town.

It was a little after eight-thirty the next morning when Sara Rowbotham parked her car outside the sexual health support service she ran in Rochdale, stepping out to see two shivering girls sitting on the steps. They had made it back to town and had been waiting there for hours. Before they were dumped on the moors the night before, both had been violently raped by several men.

As a Crisis Intervention Team Coordinator for the NHS, it was Rowbotham's work with vulnerable young girls who were being abused that began to shed light on the horrific crimes happening in Rochdale. The reports she presented to the authorities told of a sickening epidemic of sexual abuse.

She relayed details of teenage girls being plied with alcohol and coerced into unprotected intercourse with multiple men, many of whom were more than thirty years older than them. She also told of young girls being threatened and picked up in car parks and taken to houses across the town, where they would be passed around dozens of men. In one case, a man in his forties poured petrol on the head of a fourteen-year-old girl with learning difficulties and threatened to set her alight unless she performed a sexual act on him.

For too long, Rowbotham's complaints had been dismissed. She had been notifying the authorities of incidents like this since 2004, but no substantial action had been taken. It was a combination of blind prejudice and the pressures of police targets that made the authorities seemingly impervious to the horror.

On the one hand, the protective agencies judged the girls as promiscuous teenagers who were making 'lifestyle choices' by apparently 'choosing' to engage in sexual activity with these men. Even some social workers saw the girls as partly culpable for their own abuse because of 'poor decisions' they had made. In some cases, the girls had even been branded as prostitutes. Such views seeped into the ways the girls had been described: one young woman was described as dressing 'like a prostitute', another seen as indulging in 'attention-seeking behaviour'.

On the other hand, the police were being squeezed by police standards watchdogs, and were under pressure to hit 'volume targets' in bringing down acquisitive crimes such as burglary and vehicle-related thefts. This target culture meant they prioritised these kinds of crimes – and either ignored others or kicked them into the long grass. This had created a perfect storm: an environment in which girls were abused in plain sight and were then blamed for the crimes against them.

Thankfully, Sara doggedly persisted and through conversations with an officer in the Public Protection Investigations Unit, she convinced the police to carry out what they called 'disruption activity'. This saw officers knock on the doors of suspects to let the community know that the police were watching them.

A member of Sara's Crisis Intervention Team was subsequently seconded to Greater Manchester Police and was able to help officers fill in evidence gaps. The girls provided more information to identify men who had abused them, leading to the police being persuaded to revisit the case. Heading up the prosecution, I was determined that this time, we would make things right.

Detective Chief Superintendent Mary Doyle was head of public protection at Greater Manchester Police, and was as eager as us to bring the case forward. She immediately prioritised speaking to the other victims, meaning that, finally, the girls' voices were being heard.

As we proceeded, with Doyle patiently and painstakingly gathering new evidence, I was satisfied that the investigation was progressing with a greater level of professionalism, but I also knew it was going to be tough to bring forward a prosecution. Yes, there was a new investigation team; yes, we had found other potential victims; yes, we were prepared to arrest the perpetrators. However, having decided not to prosecute the ringleader and other key figures of the grooming gang back in 2009 when the original case was dismissed, how could we now say we believed Girl A? Just thinking about how that conversation would go with the jury gave me a headache. *'Members of the jury, we want you to believe the brave testimony of Girl A – even if we didn't believe her ourselves.'*

Immediately this would introduce reasonable doubt. If the prosecution and the police didn't believe this girl then, why should a jury believe her now? And if we couldn't prosecute the men in the case of Girl A, how could we press on with cases for the other girls? It presented a legal nightmare.

By now I had been a prosecutor for over twenty years, and in that time had never reversed a decision taken by another prosecutor; the legal test was simply too high. This test was one known as the Wednesbury unreasonableness, and it rules that for a decision to be overturned, it must be 'so unreasonable that no reasonable authority could ever have come to it'. Usually, the damage such a decision would do to public confidence in justice meant that it was impossible to reverse a ruling. There were only a few cases in the history of the CPS where it had happened.

For weeks, though, ever since I saw the video of Girl A, this idea had played on my mind. As I had said to my team the morning afterwards, what else could be done? I was absolutely satisfied it was the right choice. I believed the girls were telling the truth, I was adamant these men needed to be prosecuted and was sure that, contrary to the usual thinking, public confidence in justice would actually be damaged if we didn't overturn the original ruling. I informed DCS Doyle of my intention and, shortly afterwards, handed in an official notice to set things in motion. As I sat in my office with one of the team, who held the envelope containing the notice, we talked about what needed to be done next.

'It's simple,' I said. 'We do what we should have done in 2009.' I sounded confident, but we both knew it was complicated. How, my colleague asked, could we explain our dismissal of Girl A?

I leaned forward and met his gaze. 'We're going to put our hands up and say we got it wrong.'

His eyes widened. The word 'wrong' wasn't something any of us were used to saying in relation to our line of work. 'Wrong' wasn't even a word in the legal test that needed to be applied in order to reverse the 2009 decision. Nowadays, the test has changed and simply asks if the decision was wrong. At the time, however, the word used was 'unreasonable'. No one ever said they were wrong within these walls, let alone admitted such a thing to the outside world. But sometimes, in order to move forward, we needed to make difficult choices. Why should victims pay the price for our mistakes?

Once we had agreed this course of action, it was as though a weight had been lifted from our shoulders. After that things started to happen fast. The police began knocking on doors and making arrests, leading to Fran formally authorising the charging of eleven men. Only two men had been investigated in 2009, but more offenders were now known to police.

The next step was for Mary Doyle and me to decide which of the girls would be witnesses in court. There were forty-seven potential witnesses, and from that Mary and her team had narrowed the field down to under a dozen. This selection was based on the 'quality' or detail of each girl's evidence balanced against an analysis of the trauma they had experienced, and whether they were mentally fit to give evidence as a result. It would be an incredibly difficult thing for them to face, and we all knew it. We decided to bring six witnesses in the end, including Girl A. We were confident in our evidence, and we didn't want to prolong the suffering of more victims than was absolutely necessary.

It was of vital importance that we fully supported our six incredibly vulnerable victims throughout the trial. However, it didn't help that were no guidelines for how this should be done. The ones there were simply weren't fit for purpose and related to standard crimes like burglary, where people had a vested interest in the investigation taking place and felt there was likely to be justice at the end of it. They were limited guidelines to provide support, communication and information. However, the victims we were working with had no faith in the justice system, had never trusted an adult and didn't know how the justice system worked. We were using an approach that simply had no understanding of just how defenceless the witnesses were.

Given both the history of this case and our prior failings, it was going to be tough to win their trust. Most of their experience of adults was either of abusers, or police officers who had failed them. This meant communication needed to be handled delicately, if we were to build bridges. Margaret Oliver, a police officer who had been part of the team working with the girls back in the build-up to the 2009 decision, had done a lot of good work with one of the alleged victims. But this girl was despised by several of the other victims, who alleged she had acted as their pimp. If we were going to deliver justice, we needed to need to find a way of ensuring solidarity among the victims.

Oliver had now left the force, so we needed to find another officer who could build and maintain trust with the girls. Mary's team identified a well-respected liaison officer who would be in place throughout the trial, her only role being to communicate every aspect of the prosecution to the victims and give them assurance each day. She could concentrate on their wellbeing, meaning that we could focus on getting the job done.

The next step was to appoint counsel, which we did early on

so that our two barristers could begin to prepare a lengthy case. I was almost certain that the defence were going to rely on one strategy: to disrupt the procedure by applying pressure to our vulnerable victims in order to get a mistrial declared, either before or during the case. They knew, as we did, that there was no way the prosecution team would get these girls back to give evidence a second time if something like that was to occur.

One way that a defence could seek a mistrial might be if they objected to evidence that they had never seen before, in which case they might argue that they had not been given full disclosure and therefore the trial was unfair. This was something I had seen happen before. So, to protect us from this possibility, we put together a disclosure package complete with, crucially, an electronic diary. We hadn't used one before and it meant that every single piece of evidence we submitted to the defence was signed for, with a date and time. It seems simple, but was hugely important for us, meaning that there should be no 'full disclosure' argument against any of the evidence we brought to court. Our meticulous preparations didn't stop them trying, though. On more than one occasion in the pre-trial period we sent medical evidence and the defence subsequently contacted us to say they had never received anything: but we always had our confirmation of the dates and times of their receipt of the evidence. We were relentlessly fastidious.

There were plenty of other things beyond our control, of course. On the first day of the trial at Liverpool Crown Court, for example, one of the defence barristers was jostled by a far-right protester outside the court. Had that been me – and I received my fair share of abuse later on in the trial – I would have focused on the day ahead. But this barrister went into court and told the judge that because of the skirmish, his clients couldn't get a fair trial and the case must be stopped. His argument was that jurors would have to pass through this group of men shouting and screaming abuse every day and that this would play on their fears. They were meant to focus only on the evidence in the case, but if people were constantly in their faces aggressively claiming there were other issues at play, then he thought this could have an impact on their decision-making.

Fortunately, the judge was unmoved, though he did arrange for extra police officers to be stationed outside the court to reduce the risk of further aggravation. This didn't deter the defence barrister, who stood up to say he was going to withdraw because his personal safety was at risk. In my view, this was simply another attempt to get the case adjourned while a new legal team was appointed. Once again, the judge was unmoved. He had a junior barrister with him, he said, who could stand in until they found another barrister – and this was what happened. This option would not normally have been available but because of the gravity of the offence, the defence lawyers were entitled to have a junior counsel as well as the customary leading counsel. Meaning there was no shortfall, and the case could continue.

*

One of the biggest challenges of the case was always going to be the defence team's cross-examination of the girls, and so it proved. Girl A appeared via video link from a police station and was questioned by eleven barristers over a period of six days. It was exhausting enough for us, so I couldn't imagine what it must have been like for her. The defence had no other strategy than to say this didn't happen and day after day she'd be told she was a liar. When she had been questioned by the ninth barrister, she finally lost her temper – much to the barrister's delight. 'Now we see the real you!' he exclaimed.

I watched in despair. Facing such scrutiny would be gruelling for anyone and it was no surprise that, worn down in this way, a witness might lash out – particularly one who had been through so much already. How were these girls expected to give evidence for so long, to so many barristers who were all trying their best to denigrate their characters? Personally, I thought as I watched the video link, I would have snapped a long time ago.

There were twenty-four barristers and eleven solicitors in that court every day and this inevitably heightened the already charged atmosphere. I could feel my own nerves thrumming as I watched proceedings. I was grateful that at least the girls had extensive support, including their own independent sexual violence advisors who provided pre-trial therapy and sexual violence counselling. Our police liaison officer would also visit often to try and put them at ease. With one of the witnesses, for example, she would wake her up with a bacon sandwich and put on a Disney film for her. Anything to try and maintain some semblance of normality and get them through this ordeal.

Eventually, the girls finished giving their evidence and the judge had to decide if there was a case to answer. If he didn't deem the evidence strong enough, then he wouldn't let the case go to the jury. At this point, the jury had left the court while we made a five-minute submission to the judge stating why we felt the case should proceed. The defence argued vociferously that there were so many contradictions in what the girls were saying that there was no way any jury could reasonably expect to convict. Thankfully, the judge sided with our opposing argument and declared there was a case to answer.

A major obstacle was out of the way. The jury returned and once the defendants started to give their evidence, I began to relax a little. One of the things about trials with multiple defendants is that they can be good for the prosecution: the defendants often end up stabbing each other in the back. Once an individual is under pressure and can feel the prospect of a heavy jail sentence getting closer, they try and shift the blame to another defendant.

It wasn't me. I didn't do it, it was him.

I'd seen this many times before and it always had the same effect: it made all the defendants seem guilty. That was certainly the case in this courtroom.

Our barristers vigorously cross-examined all the defendants over the best part of a month and while their defence was weak, it didn't pass without incident. At one point, while one of the defendants was being cross-examined he suddenly appeared to faint, and paramedics had to be called in. The married father of five had previously claimed that he thought the fifteen-year-old girl he had sex with was in her late twenties. Another defendant removed his shirt as he stood in the dock and tore out clumps of his own chest hair to try and demonstrate that he would have left follicles of his hair at the scene of his crimes. He dismissed the accusations as 'white lies' and shouted abuse at the judge, jury and police.

None of it was edifying. It was sickening, in fact, and as we approached closing speeches, I felt confident about our chances of success. We had, I was sure, withstood everything the defence had to throw at us. But it's never over until it's over, and at this late stage it would transpire that there remained a threat to the trial. And it was to come from an unexpected source.

By now it was May 2012, and the case was coming to an end around the time of local elections, so we shouldn't have been too surprised that someone might try to make some political capital from the trial. But it still came as a shock when we saw the leader of the BNP, Nick Griffin, tweet the following verdict a few days after the jury had retired to make their decision.

'News flash. Seven of the Muslim paedophile rapists found guilty in Liverpool.'

As soon as I saw this, my heart sank. People would think

Griffin had someone on the inside giving him information. How else could he know the jury's decision before it had been made? He hadn't said all or even simply 'some' of those on trial had been found guilty. He'd tweeted a specific number and it could bring the whole case down. The judge would be under pressure to investigate, because the defence could argue that there was a leak and that the jury was biased. Sure enough, the defence immediately called for a mistrial on the basis that the BNP had a mole in the jury.

The judge called the jury foreman and asked him if any of the jurors had had conversations about the case outside of the jury room. He responded in the negative. Each member of the jury in turn was called forward, interviewed, and asked the same question. All denied speaking about the case to anyone, other than their fellow jurors within their appointed room, where all electronic equipment is banned and jurors are closely monitored. The police, meanwhile, established that Griffin had tweeted while the jury was in this room. How, then, could he have got to them?

Back in the room where the judge had called a meeting, eleven lawyers and the jury sat tight. The judge hadn't finished his investigation. He frowned pensively and stood up. He still had one more question for the jury.

'Have you reached a verdict yet?' the judge asked the foreman. 'What is your view at the moment?'

'Yes,' answered the foreman. 'We have found seven defendants guilty.'

This was exactly the result that Nick Griffin had tweeted. My heart sank to my boots.

The defence lawyers present immediately ratcheted up pressure on the judge and the police moved to question Griffin, who had already subsequently backtracked on his tweet. When interviewed by the police, he said he didn't have any information from the jury and had simply guessed the number of guilty verdicts. He claimed he had had no intention of prejudicing the jury. It just so happened that his guess was correct.

Eventually, the judge was satisfied no jurors were at fault. They had, he said, taken a 'perfectly reasonable, logical and unbiased approach to the evidence' and there was no evidence of communication with the BNP. Shortly afterwards, the jury would return with their guilty verdicts.

Of course, I was delighted to be on the verge of seeing these men convicted, giving the girls the justice they deserved. But now, just before the jury returned, there was another narrative developing outside the courtroom, bringing new scrutiny. The media were beginning to look at the institutional failure in the initial dealings with this case.

With the jury still out, we were preparing for a pre-verdict briefing with the media. This meant we had prepared a response to both outcomes, but the media were more interested in why we hadn't acted previously when we had been presented with evidence of these crimes. This was going to come up regardless of the outcome.

CPS headquarters had put together what I called a 'blah blah' press statement, in that it said very little and included no mention of our decision not to prosecute the case in 2009, even though our press office was taking calls constantly from journalists who were asking precisely this question. The aim of the CPS was to avoid more controversy, to try and put the case to bed, and I could sympthasise – no one wanted to open themselves up to criticism if they could possibly avoid it, and perhaps the thinking was that our success in prosecuting these men would somehow make everyone forget about our previous failures. I simply didn't agree. The only way to move on, I had always felt, was to be completely honest about what had gone before, and to show the public that we could recognise our errors and correct them.

I didn't want the attention taken away from my colleague John Dilworth, in charge of the prosecution for my team and the one who would be addressing the media. But I wanted to prepare him as best as I could, so I amended the CPS statement to reference the 2009 decision. We had to deal with it upfront.

The next day, journalists from across the country assembled for the briefing at Greater Manchester Police headquarters. John sat at the table at the front for the CPS along with Assistant Chief Constable Steve Heywood for the police and Jim Taylor, the Chief Executive of Rochdale Council. I sat at the back of the room, in the audience. Having been in the pre-briefing I knew there was a well-prepared script, which would focus on successful prosecutions and justice being delivered. Of course, no journalist was interested in this. The media wanted the other story.

'So what happened in 2009? Why was no one prosecuted then?' asked one journalist, when it was time for questions.

I could see John sinking down into his seat. None of them wanted to deal with this, which seemed rather naive to me. The panel kept attempting to bat away this line of questioning, and the atmosphere in the room quickly became fraught. *'Can't you just answer the question?'*

I couldn't keep watching, doing nothing, keeping silent. I found myself getting to my feet. The room turned to look at me, standing at the back of the audience.

'I'm Nazir Afzal,' I said, in the sudden hush. 'I'm the Chief Crown Prosecutor for the North West and I can tell you that decisions were taken in 2009 by police and prosecutors not to prosecute this case. Those decisions were wrong.' Now the room was completely silent. 'When I arrived in May last year, I reversed that decision, which is why we can now focus on justice being done.'

It's hard to admit to mistakes, particularly when vulnerable people had suffered so much as a result, and when you also knew that your colleagues may face consequences. Ultimately, both the police and the CPS would issue apologies for their failures. Thirteen police officers would be investigated, social workers struck off, council officers cleared out and 'improvement notices' issued. The Chief Constable of Greater Manchester Police would go on to announce that child sexual exploitation was the force's number one priority. It was tough for all of us, but if we were to do our jobs properly, we needed to make ourselves vulnerable, to humble ourselves and recognise when we could do better.

Later, I was pacing around my office in Manchester, looking at my phone and waiting anxiously for news of the verdict. I couldn't settle until I had it. Finally, the phone rang.

'Nine are guilty,' John announced.

For the first time in a long time, I smiled.

The nine were jailed soon afterwards for up to twenty-five years each and outside the court a statement from one of the victims was read out to relay her 'brilliant relief'. It was something we all shared. 'After all these years something had been done,' she said. I felt those words deep in my bones. Something *had* been done. And the whole world knew about it. David Cameron would even call me, asking me how widespread a problem these grooming gangs were. I relayed the earlier failures of the case, along with the additional fact that the crime itself was a deep-rooted problem that we simply hadn't been paying enough attention to nationwide. It was the first time we had ever prosecuted internal trafficking in this country and we were finally tackling a problem that had been hidden for too long. It certainly wasn't a problem unique to the north of England. So it proved: within a year of the trial, grooming gangs were being prosecuted on Cameron's doorstep in Oxford.

Reflecting on the trial in the following days, my mind came back to the same problems that often troubled me: not only the question of institutional change, and reforming our agencies to make them fit for purpose, but also the underlying cultural issues that created the crime itself. As always, we needed to do more with the communities committing these crimes, to try and drive cultural change.

In the aftermath of the case, I would sit on many panels discussing these crimes. One of them was a Rochdale Community Forum, which had been set up by a local Imam and was supported by police, community groups, the council and faith groups. It aimed to shine a light on sexual crimes in the community and as I arrived at Rochdale town hall, I knew that while the community was still hurting, we couldn't avoid uncomfortable truths.

As I took to the podium, I cleared my throat and looked out at the audience. I had no script – I found I always spoke more convincingly without one – but I had a serious message to deliver.

'These failings can't simply be laid at the door of the police and social services,' I began. 'Some of you would have known what was going on. Some of you might have seen it happening, and some of you would have heard about it. It beggars belief that a fifty-nine-year-old Asian man can be driving around all the time with a fourteen-year-old white girl in the back of the car and nobody noticed.'

I paused, watching a man stand up from his seat.

'So, do you want us to be a grass then? You want us all to be whistleblowers?'

'I want us to be good neighbours,' I responded.

The silence in the room told me I had touched a nerve. I could understand the apprehension and confusion in the community, which feared reprisals from the far right. Stephen Yaxley-Lennon, aka Tommy Robinson, had recently addressed an English Defence League march in the area, and Asian taxi drivers were being attacked. One taxi firm had even launched a policy of offering white drivers on request. I also knew from my own early life that there was a mistrust of the police in these communities, and that people often felt that justice was not present in their spaces.

My job was to provide reassurance that this was not an attack on the British-Pakistani community, but an attack on perpetrators hiding among them, who damaged the community with their actions. Yet I also wanted to make it absolutely clear that we would prosecute these crimes relentlessly: no fear, no favour.

I soon became aware that I was also ruffling feathers on the far right by their having been unable to capitalise fully on this case precisely because of my involvement. A brown-skinned person having reversed the decision not to prosecute, brought the case to court and seen nine members of a grooming gang jailed: it seriously damaged their narrative. They wanted to say the CPS were protecting Asian criminals and allowing the rape of innocent white girls. As long as I was seen to be responsible for prosecuting these criminals, their story lost all its power.

Nevertheless, their fervour remained. Meanwhile, the press continued to circle, wanting to know more about the identities of the prosecutors who had blocked the case back in 2009. This put me in a difficult position.

Of course, I knew who they were. One had already left the CPS and the other had been disciplined. But I wasn't going to hang them out to dry: while I was happy to talk about our institutional failure, I didn't want to destroy lives. I told journalists that I took responsibility for anything that happened in the CPS, even the things that hadn't happened on my watch. We had to accept that we were institutionally responsible.

Perhaps this played into the hands of the far right. Suddenly, they had been given a chance to resurrect their failed narrative: they could place the blame on me personally. Their Facebook groups exploded into life with claims that it was Nazir Afzal who didn't prosecute the Rochdale Asian grooming gangs in 2009. It was my first taste of fake news and, given it was so patently false, I was surprised that it took hold and stuck. My inbox was under siege from their vile messages. Within forty-eight hours, 17,000 abusive and racist emails had poured into my personal inbox demanding that I be sacked and deported, and my staff were also getting the same messages.

It wasn't only messages. The police warned me that there had been threats to my safety. An officer came to my house and installed a panic alarm, methodically running my family through how to use it in the event of an attack. It was a terrible experience. How had I got to the point where my wife and children were suddenly in danger? My kids were scared and my wife wanted to know what was going on. It was a question I simply couldn't answer: I couldn't predict the pattern of their hatred. All I knew was that I had done the right thing.

That weekend, a group of men congregated in the cul-de-sac where I lived, armed with placards and banners calling me an apologist for rape gangs. As I lifted the phone to call the police, I could feel my hands shaking: anger surged through me, more intense than anything I had ever felt. I had spent twenty years prosecuting some of the worst criminals in the country. I'd been exposed to rapists, murderers, terrorists. I'd seen the worst of humanity. But I never talked about my work at home. I always left it at the office, kept it separate from my family. Now, it was invading my personal life and threatening those I loved the most.

The next day, a police officer was stationed outside the house.

'The Prime Minister has a police officer outside his door too,' I said gently to the kids, trying to reassure them. The police had advised that our children shouldn't walk to school anymore, so for several weeks we sent them in a taxi.

For the first time, I felt we were prisoners in our own home. My home had always been my sanctuary, and now it felt violated. I was constantly looking behind me, expecting a BNP protester to burst into my meetings or follow me down the street. It reminded me of being a boy on the streets of Birmingham, on the run from thugs.

Mostly I was just devastated that I couldn't protect my children. They could go online and see every vile thing that had been written.

'Why are they saying this about you, Dad? Why are they telling lies?'

I didn't know how to answer.

Child grooming had fully established itself in the public consciousness as an abhorrent, highly emotive crime. Unfortunately, extremists saw an opportunity in it to exploit for their own ends the visceral anger felt by millions. If they managed to disrupt police grooming investigations and cause cases to collapse, then their rallying cry about there being no justice because of a failed establishment would resonate loudly and start winning hearts and minds. It would inspire a new kind of vigilante justice, which would in turn spark a violent street revolution. Discrediting law and order was what would enable their poisonous ideology to take hold.

The more I thought about it, the more it worried me. Why? Because I knew that, in a way, their message would have appealed to my younger self. As a teenager I was told there was no justice, and the world I grew up in reinforced this. There would be many others who felt the same, no matter what the colour of the skin. Whatever was going on at home, I knew I needed to keep working.

I was spending long days at the CPS, consulting with my boss Keir Starmer (who had replaced Ken Macdonald as Director of Public Prosecutions in 2008) on what we needed to do in the wake of Rochdale. We had learned a lot, and I felt cautiously optimistic that we could apply the lessons successfully. We began to develop the Child Sexual Abuse Review Panel, which would look at instances where previously dismissed cases of sexual abuse could be re-examined, should a victim wish to revisit their allegations.

It is not always possible to establish where the truth lies, but when it is possible there must be good reason not to do so. The position of a complainant whose allegation is described as 'unsubstantiated' is extraordinarily difficult, but sometimes 'unsubstantiated' is in reality a euphemism for 'un-investigated'.

The panel opened the floodgates for the investigation of historic sexual crimes. One individual success of our work was it eventually leading to the conviction of football coach Barry Bennell for subjecting young players at Manchester City and Crewe to hundreds of sexual offences. He was jailed for thirty years.

The more long-term success was that the work of the panel led in due course to the Metropolitan Police launching Operation Yewtree. It was a watershed moment and the nation was about to have to deal with some deeply uncomfortable truths surfacing about a host of prominent celebrities, some until then widely beloved. Sir Jimmy Savile was exposed as a prolific sex offender and Stuart Hall, Gary Glitter and Rolf Harris were all jailed for sexual abuse. The right of powerful people to abuse people from lower social classes, seemingly impervious to justice, was over. A dirty secret in Rochdale that had been ignored for too long had given us the impetus to look hard at Britain's landscape of sexual abuse.

We had to do more than just prioritise this crime in our prosecutions, though. We had to make justice more accessible, make it easier for victims to give evidence and ensure that protective agencies were properly trained to spot signs of grooming.

To achieve this, the courts had to change. Victims such as Girl A shouldn't have to experience multiple cross examinations over many days. Discussions began with the CPS policy leads, court services and judiciary leads to establish what would become known as the 'ground rules' hearing, where judges would meet with representatives from both the prosecution and the defence before a case to set parameters for the fair treatment of vulnerable defendants and vulnerable witnesses.

Nor could Britain continue to have forty-three police forces each having their own different way of tackling child sexual abuse: an inconsistent approach inevitably meant victims would suffer. Some forces had no guidelines on how to investigate cases of child sexual abuse; others had nothing specific for children and relied on general rape and sexual offences guidelines. This wasn't good enough. To remedy it, we created the first ever national guidelines for prosecutors and, working with the Chief Constable who was the national police lead for CSA (child sexual abuse) and the College of Policing, developed a set of guidelines for all police forces in the country.

Another new guideline ensured that judges were to be specially trained to deal with cases of CSA. This was extended to the police, and a course was created for specialist child sexual abuse officers to guarantee they were trained and accredited in the same way as specialist firearms officers. The same applied to prosecutors, and I became the national lead for a network of specialist prosecutors up and down the country. We were overhauling the system.

The courts had serious work heading their way and they had to be ready. In the summer of 2012 the Deputy Children's Commissioner, Sue Berelowitz, issued a report stating that child abuse wasn't just taking place in inner cities, as was often assumed to be the case. It was happening everywhere and social networking sites, as well as easy-to-access pornography, were fuelling the problem. The Prime Minister finally had his answer to the question about how widespread this crime was. Who knew how many childhoods had been destroyed? We would never discover the full truth but we could work to remedy the mistakes of the past, and to protect the victims of the future.

I look back now and see that the Rochdale grooming trial was one of the most important cases not only in my career, but in the history of modern British justice.

X

In the early years of the twenty-first century, a great tide of modernity swept through Britain. Landmark legislation came in the form of Civil Partnerships, the Equality Act and the Human Rights Act. These changes were meant to signify a clean break with an old and divided society. It was, as Tony Blair explained, a time 'for sweeping away all the detritus of the past'.

Yet once you scratch the veneer of civilisation, it didn't take long to reveal an altogether different society to this modern, more enlightened one we were supposedly becoming. Indeed, Britain today continues to be plagued by uncomfortable truths and is far from the 'nation at ease with itself' that John Major once envisaged.

As powerful as that tide of change was, there were many crimes that the new legislation did not touch, crimes which clung resolutely to Britain's underbelly and that the authorities simply didn't know about, let alone understand. In my career I had already seen honour killings and a child sexual exploitation epidemic brought into the light. But there was another crime being overlooked, and it was one that most people thought no longer existed in Britain. It was the oldest form of exploitation, taking new and modern forms: slavery.

A report by the Joseph Rowntree Foundation in 2007 acknowledged that while there were no reliable statistics on the extent of modern slavery in the UK, they could confidently assert that thousands of children were being trafficked into the country for this purpose. The report noted that the government tended to address trafficking as an issue of migration rather than human rights, and called for a more robust stance against the exploiters. Since the 2004 Asylum and Immigration Act, it observed, there had yet to be a single prosecution brought for trafficking for labour exploitation.

Those leading this exploitation were largely gangmasters, and there were said to be thousands of them in the UK. The 2004 Morecambe Bay cockling disaster had shocked the nation with the reality of hideous exploitation that had until then been hidden in plain sight. Twenty-three Chinese cockle pickers drowned that day, trapped by tides on the Lancashire coast. This case brought the crime to public attention, but it was just the tip of the iceberg. From factories and farms to nail bars and car washes, the authorities were beginning to realise just how vast a problem trafficking for labour exploitation was in the UK and how little was being done to prevent it. There was a huge lack of awareness on the part of crime agencies and the protections to prevent workers from being exploited in supply chains were wholly inadequate.

I was used to dealing with vulnerable victims. But what I didn't know then, as I leafed through fledgling research on slavery in Britain, was that I was about to come across the most vulnerable victim I'd ever encountered. Her story would stay with me, would mark me perhaps more than any other I had worked on.

I will call her Safiya.

It was June 2000. At Heathrow Airport, a young girl blinked in the early morning light. She had slept for a long time, woken only as she was dragged through arrivals. This is what she remembers:

She felt as though she was in a bad dream. Everything seemed utterly alien. She didn't know it, but England had just been knocked out of the European Championship and the dejected people with Saint George's flags wrapped around their waists who trudged past her were fans on their way home. People in strange clothes swarmed around, while a team of dogs sniffed at luggage and a woman slowly mopped the floor. The smell of detergent was thick in the air; it made her feel sick.

A man had sat beside her on the plane, and it was he who gripped her shoulder and pushed her forwards as they approached border control. On her other side, her wrist was in the tight clasp of a woman. Neither spoke to her. A man in a blue uniform at the desk studied some documents. He looked at her. His mouth was moving and the man and woman leaned in close to him. But, as had happened so often, Safiya couldn't tell what was passing between them. This was because she was deaf, and couldn't hear anything at all. Her heart was thumping, and she searched her pockets for the small rag doll she always carried. It wasn't there.

After a few moments the man in blue finally nodded, and the three of them were allowed to pass. From the arrivals hall she stepped out into the cold British air. The man and woman bundled her into a car and the next thing she knew they were driving very fast down a wide road. The vibrations made her body tremble as she stared out at the unfamiliar landscape, so different to the narrow, dusty streets she knew in Lahore.

She stole a glance at the woman who sat beside her in the back seat. Her face was stern and her eyes dark with kohl. The woman turned to catch her staring and slapped her hard across the face. Safiya recoiled and cowered by the window, trying to make sense of what was happening. Where were her parents, she wondered? What was she doing in this place? She was so exhausted from her long journey that, despite her fear, she found herself drifting back into a deep sleep.

When she awoke, her face was pressed against a cold floor and her whole body was shivering. Where she had been struck on her cheek ached with pain. There was no light in the room, it was completely dark. Safiya felt her way round the room until she found a door, but it was locked.

Crawling to the corner of the room, she discovered a small, hard bed and climbed on top, curling up to keep warm. Then she waited.

After what seemed like several hours, a light clicked on, revealing to Safiya the rest of the small, spartan room – a makeshift desk, a chair and the little bed were its only contents. As she blinked to take everything in, the door opened. In the doorway stood the man and woman who'd pushed her through the airport.

The woman stood next to her and stared. Her dark eyes showed no emotion. Safiya could sense violence in her, and at that moment the bruise on her cheek seemed to throb, a reminder of what the woman could do. The man was tall and imposing with a neatly trimmed grey beard. He too showed no sign of kindness, no sign of warmth. Only cruelty. They beckoned to her and she stepped forward, despite her fear. Anything was better than that cold, dark room. She was led up a staircase to the main room of what seemed to Safiya to be a large house. From the front window she could see a driveway, a wrought-iron gate and, beyond, cars parked in an orderly fashion down the street.

She turned back to look at her captor; his face was contorted with anger and he threw his arms up as if in frustration. Safiya wished she knew what was happening when his mouth moved, but her world was utterly quiet. Her silence was too much for him and he lunged forward and grabbed Safiya's hair, pulling her into the kitchen where he and the woman used a series of gestures to explain to her what she would be required to do.

Over the next few days, Safiya learned what was expected of her. She would cook, wash, sew, iron and clean the house. The cold, dark room in which she had awoken was a cellar, and it was where they kept her when she wasn't working – which wasn't often. The days were long and if she slowed or her attention wavered, retribution was swift and severe. Both adults would kick, punch and slap her. On other occasions they would grab her hair and bang her head against the walls until she bled. In the kitchen she was attacked with a rolling pin and beaten savagely with a cooking pot. That time, she wiped the blood from her eyes and continued to wash the dishes.

Safiya might not be able to hear them, but her captors had devised their own communication system. They flicked the lights of her cellar on and off when she was needed. She was expected to respond immediately: to ignore them, or be too slow, was to risk another beating. If she wanted to use the toilet while locked in the cellar, she had to bang on the door until someone came and released her. Sometimes they didn't come at all. If she did manage to make it to the toilet, she was often thrown down the stairs back to her cellar room. Safiya never saw any payment and lived off a meagre diet of leftovers.

The physical scars began to add up, as did the months and years. She saw little of the outside world, and didn't even know what country she was in. Her twelfth birthday came and went, and soon she was a teenager. Then she was fourteen, then fifteen. The year 2005 arrived, and Britain hosted the G8 Summit. Hundreds of thousands attended a rally in a show of solidarity with the world's poorest people. A compère climbed on stage, shouting to the crowd that they had made slavery history and they could make poverty history too.

But slavery was not history, not for Safiya. A few miles from where Safiya was held as a slave in a Salford cellar, staff filed into the Equality and Human Rights Commission each day. Less than five miles away from where she was imprisoned stood a statue of Abraham Lincoln in Manchester city centre. It marked the support and sacrifices made by Manchester cotton workers during the American Civil War to bring about the abolition of slavery.

Safiya didn't scream – she had never learned to speak, because of being deaf as well as because of the neglect she suffered – but it never stopped her trying. At night she would lie awake, scrunch her eyes closed, and force the air out of her lungs. There were other moments when she was beyond screaming: in these moments she was paralysed with shock and pain. She learned to expect the door to open in the middle of the night. Then, the man with the beard climbed into her bed.

Safiya had become accustomed to violence and had learned to move quickly in order to survive. But she wasn't quick enough to dodge a knife.

One day when she was cooking, she ladled some dhal to her mouth to taste. She was starving and even though she knew there would be hell to pay if she were caught, she was too hungry to care. But she had failed to notice someone looming behind her. When she finally sensed the presence, it was already too late. The woman knocked her to the ground and grabbed her hair as she pushed her face down to meet Safiya's. Her eyes pulsed with fury and as Safiya struggled to break free, a kitchen knife was forced into her midriff. A halo of blood circled the white kitchen tiles. She was lifted up and the last thing she remembered before passing out was the agony of her wounds being roughly bandaged.

Safiya survived without going to hospital and, as soon as she was sufficiently recovered, the beatings and sexual abuse continued. Her life was a succession of violence, submission and obedience. While the march of human rights progress continued for the rest of the country, the age-old problem of slavery was left behind. Safiya had little chance of ever escaping. She was completely invisible.

But not, it would appear, to everyone.

By now Safiya's work had expanded. Her captors had branched out into selling counterfeit goods and Safiya would spend hours packing football shirts, clothes and phone covers from her prison. Meanwhile, a lucrative business was developing, and an extensive range of counterfeit goods was being distributed through markets and shops across Manchester.

It was this that attracted the attention of the police. For a decade Safiya's captors had kept her hidden away, but they were about to find they could no longer operate under a cloak of invisibility. Manchester was fast becoming the country's counterfeit capital and police were starting to crack down on the back alleys and basements behind Strangeways Prison, where many knock-off brands were sold. In June 2009, Trading Standards had traced some of this activity back to the house in which Safiya was imprisoned – and eventually they came knocking on the door, with a warrant to search the premises.

Once inside, officers noticed a locked door, behind which were the stairs leading to the cellar. Turning to the man with the beard, they demanded he surrender the keys. After much protesting, he reluctantly handed them over. The door unlocked, officers stooped and went down into the cellar, expecting to find boxes of counterfeit goods. Instead they found a slight, mute young woman. That day, several members of the family that had trafficked her into the UK were arrested and Safiya was taken into custody where police attempted to interview her with the help of a sign language translator.

Officers could tell just by looking at the trembling young woman before them that she had been exploited. Safiya's clothes were threadbare, she was underweight and bruises were visible. What they didn't know at the time was exactly what had happened, and she didn't have the language to tell them. Slowly, painstakingly, the police began to put the pieces together and, when they did, it wasn't long before Safiya's case came to my attention.

Her case was directly raised with me by a fellow prosecutor and police lead during a training course at the CPS offices in London. Because of my experience with exceptionally vulnerable witnesses, they sought my advice on putting a case together, and I was happy to help.

I listened intently as they recounted the case. I had years of experience as a prosecutor and sometimes it felt like I had dealt with every case in the criminal repertoire. But this was different. When the prosecutor had finished telling Safiya's story, I was astonished and appalled. I had never known anyone so vulnerable, so alone, facing so many obstacles not only in her own life but in the criminal proceedings we were planning to bring. I knew immediately it would be an extremely difficult case; there was so little in the way of evidence. Everything relied on her. She would be the one to have to prove she had been kept as a slave. Yet how could she do that given her circumstances and disabilities? How could she share her experiences? It would be a tough job for anyone but would surely be near impossible for someone who had been so abused and lacked the ability to hear or speak.

As I drove home that night, I thought of nothing else. How could we get Safiya's case to a courtroom and how could we help her to provide the best evidence? It was going to take a long time to get this to trial and the vast amount of support she needed was almost certainly going to cause us problems.

Because it was her word against theirs, the defence would be planning to accuse the prosecution of manipulating the witness. There was no doubt about it: this was a prosecution that could definitely fail. But I couldn't get Safiya out of my mind.

The next morning, as soon as I was in the office, I gathered the prosecution team together to discuss Safiya's case. Concerns were immediately raised about the impact the trial could have on her. Prosecution must always weigh the interests of the victim with the wider interests of the public at large, and some decisions are extraordinarily sensitive and finely balanced. We sometimes decide not to prosecute cases, for example, where proceedings may cause further trauma and emotional damage to the victim. In such instances, the best result can be that the victim is moved to safety and supported by the police with a new life and identity.

On top of this, there was also a good chance we could lose, given the challenging conditions. I had to hear these doubts from my team. A voice in the back of my mind, however, told me we had to take a chance. I had long known there was a deep culture of slavery across South Asia and had often suspected it would soon be imported here. I knew that slave auctions happened in some countries such as India and Libya and I was aware that in Pakistan alone, there are around two million people in bonded slavery. It may be illegal there, but with no care system and widespread poverty, the practice is often tolerated – even sometimes accepted as the norm. We needed to make it extremely clear that slavery was not tolerated in the UK and never would be. Safiya wasn't alone. There would be others out there who needed our help.

If Safiya could give evidence, I said, we had every chance of success. I desperately wanted to proceed with the case. But where to begin? The starting point in putting our case together was accepting we were all a long way out of our comfort zone. Police officers tend to work by the book – they have their national guidelines, their charging manuals, their PACE codes of practice. We also have our code for Crown Prosecutors. Everyone is usually either working by the book or looking back to previous cases for a sense of how best to proceed. Neither option was open to us here. There had never been a case like this before, and there was no book to guide us. We were going to have to get creative and think laterally.

It had taken the police months to build up a means of communication with Safiya, and start to establish some understanding. We were able to work out the year of her birth following examination by a forensic anthropologist and odontologist. It was determined that Safiya was only ten when she had arrived in the UK from Pakistan, having been sold by her parents to the traffickers who brought her to the UK.

It was exceptionally hard going but week by week, progress was being made. This in itself was remarkable, considering everything she had been through. For the first ten years of her life she had been with a family who saw her as a burden and wanted to be rid of her. Then for the next ten she had been with a family who violently abused her and kept her as a slave. She had only ever known cruelty. So it was more than understandable that now, sat before a team of officers and a sign language translator, surrounded by their serious faces, she seemed nervous.

Safiya had begun to learn a form of sign language and multiple agencies were mobilising around her. Health professionals, translators, trauma counsellors, a police liaison officer, a registered intermediary, the adult services of her local council, the benefits team and people from the women's refuge, where she was now staying, had all been put in place to help her. They saw the scars from the kitchen knife, and learned how her captors had used her as a vehicle to claim benefits fraudulently and, most depressingly, they uncovered a litany of failings showing how she came to be allowed into the country in the first place.

Safiya, meanwhile, was getting used to her new environment and struggling with something that she had never been able to feel before, something she had never had reason to feel before: trust.

She shifted uncomfortably in her chair as light flooded through the blinds, and looked at the omelette and mug of tea placed in front of her. Nervously, she cupped her hands around the mug to feel its warmth. Tentatively picking up her fork, she looked timidly up at the adults in the room, as if to ask permission to eat.

I, on the other hand, was wrestling with an altogether different emotion. I was furious, and the further the investigation proceeded, the more reason I had to feel so. Incredibly, it emerged that when Safiya had arrived in the UK aged ten, her fake passport had said she was twenty. I couldn't believe it. How could she have been passed off as a twenty-year-old when she was a full decade younger? Moreover, how on earth could she – or her captors – have possibly provided convincing evidence to an Entry Clearance Officer to meet the necessary visa criteria? When Safiya arrived at Heathrow, immigration officers should have completed an interview with her to check her visa had been issued for the correct purpose. They also should have carried out a face-to-passport check. If they had recognised she wasn't an adult when her passport stated she was, they could have overturned her visa. Why didn't they? I did not believe for a second that this would have been an easy mistake to make.

At the time Heathrow had a Minors' Team, trained to deal with children encountered at the border – and yet somehow, they missed a child being trafficked under their nose. Records show an immigration officer even amended Safiya's boarding card to include her date of birth in order to show that she was twenty. Looking at the tiny, frightened child in front of him, he still satisfied himself that she was qualified for entry into the UK. Safiya's Case Review would eventually conclude that a combination of 'heavy workloads', a 'lack of awareness of child trafficking for domestic servitude and sexual exploitation' and 'issues of assumptions on the basis of race or culture' was behind the fact that numerous agencies failed to recognise Safiya as a vulnerable child.

But this was only half of it. Immigration officers, housing benefit visiting officers, GPs and NHS staff came into contact with Safiya and all failed to see the vulnerable, trafficked child in front of them. Apparently not one of them had spotted that she wasn't an adult, despite the fact she weighed five stone and was four foot tall when she arrived in Britain. 'It seems possible that a lack of confidence about issues of race and culture may have inhibited some professionals asking too many questions,' her Case Review would later suggest.

On other occasions the nature of what was going on was glaringly obvious – and still, public servants failed to spot it. Safiya's captors submitted immigration documents to the Home Office to try and obtain indefinite leave for her to remain in the UK. They included a section on Safiya's employment rights, which was so strangely worded it should have raised the alarm immediately. The document stated that her employer would ensure 'you do not engage in sex with any member of the household without your consent' and 'you are not locked up or kept indoors against your will'. Incredibly, the Public Enquiry Officer who dealt with this raised no questions about the nature of the employer/employee relationship evoked by this strange document.

To begin to comprehend some of this wilful blindness, it's necessary to look at Britain's political and cultural landscape in the early 2000s. In 1999, after an inquiry into the Metropolitan Police's handling of the murder of Stephen Lawrence, the Macpherson Report resulted in a long overdue, and seismic, shift in policing. It concluded that the police were 'institutionally racist' and argued that a racial incident should be defined as one that is 'perceived to be racist by the victim or by any other person'. This had huge ramifications. There was now recognition that institutions could be racist as well as individuals. This was of course a necessary step, and was long overdue, but it did also mean that there was a sudden fear of an accusation of institutional racism. Consequently, agencies were averting their eyes from the things that were wrong because they didn't want to be accused of being racist, and I believe it was this attitude that was responsible for allowing Safiya's captors to navigate a safe path through successive checkpoints and avoid the scrutiny that should have protected her. I had seen other examples of this, and it pained me every time I came across such incompetence.

Safiya, meanwhile, continued to respond well to the support she was receiving and had now learned sufficient sign language to communicate some aspects of her ordeal. The police were confident she would be able to give evidence in court. It had taken two years of remarkable multi-agency work to get a full account from her. This length of time, however, had in itself presented a phenomenal challenge, requiring me to use much ingenuity to extend the period of bail for her captors.

Initially, the CPS kept re-bailing the defendants on the basis that we were still considering the evidence. After obtaining Safiya's evidence, we next kept re-bailing on the basis that the Department of Work and Pensions had yet to give us all their data and evidence, as the police were still investigating the counterfeit operation. We also informed the courts that we were still seeking evidence from her home country and immigration authorities, and that we were struggling to find a registered intermediary who was available for the length of time the case would take.

All of this helped to buy us time. Even once we had charged Safiya's captors, we continued to watch the clock. We served our evidence in small portions, rather than in one instalment. Every time the defence asked for something, we would request an adjournment to obtain that evidence. Everything we did was about buying time for Safiya. Throughout, we were always hoping for the unlikely: that the defendants would plead guilty. Safiya would not be required to give evidence in those circumstances and so would be protected from having to go to court. This didn't happen, but the court was persuaded to give us the latest date possible for trial – it was necessary, we said, for Safiya to have as much time as she needed to be prepared. And it was the truth.

Putting together the case was extremely challenging, as we needed a decade's worth of detail from her. Safiya's first account was sketchy, but as our intermediary built a rapport with her, we began to get a fuller picture and she would eventually give police fourteen video-recorded interviews about her ordeal over all those years.

I correctly suspected she had been sexually assaulted, but we could only approach this subject towards the end of our interviews. I suspected, having dealt with so many honour-related cases, that she was likely to avoid disclosing such painful details, because she may well be feeling deep shame, blaming herself for having damaged her family's honour. We took a carefully planned and staggered approach, extracting information gradually as we tried to establish the dates of specific offences. This was virtually impossible, given the situation she had been in. We had to ask her what the weather was like outside when she was assaulted to get a sense of what season it had been. Pinning down exact dates simply wasn't going to be possible.

The effects the gruelling hours of court might have on Safiya were another concern for me. We couldn't have a session that started at 10am. and went on until 4pm, with Safiya under stress for days at a time. Our team approached Judge Peter Lakin and presented some expert testimony that suggested that Safiya would only be able to give evidence for a couple of hours a day at most. He was persuaded by the medical advice. For this case, he agreed that the court would only sit for two hours a day when Safiya was giving evidence.

And so began the longest case I had ever been involved in. It had already taken two and a half years to get Safiya's case to trial and it would go on to last for six months, making legal history for the amount of time a victim of sexual abuse gave evidence in the witness box, with Safiya spending an incredible forty-nine days there. Week after week I would gaze in awe at her giving evidence via video link in Manchester Crown

Court. It was truly remarkable seeing this diminutive woman, flanked by a panoply of support services, telling her story through sign language.

The judge had told me before the case began that he was retiring after this trial and I was beginning to wonder if it would be my last case too, if we lost. This trial had cost four times more than any other I had worked on, and the authorities were watching closely. As a prosecutor, my sole focus was to get to half time, to allow Safiya to give her evidence so we could get the accused in the witness box. But as usual the defence barristers were throwing everything they had at Safiya, trying to undermine her story.

Safiya stood firm, though, and was radiating confidence. As we were all beginning to sweat, the irony was that she became the calmest person in court. Police had described her as a 'butterfly coming out of a chrysalis' and I felt privileged to witness this transformation. On each day that she appeared, she was ready for them. Her body language had changed. The defence barristers recognised this as well, which is why they changed tack and started to probe at Safiya's intermediary.

Intermediaries were introduced in 2008 to help children and adults with communication difficulties give coherent and accurate evidence during police interviews and criminal proceedings. They are invaluable, but must stay impartial and neutral – their first duty is to the court. Our intermediary was understandably close to Safiya, having spent the last two and a half years working closely with her on a daily basis to enable her to give evidence. The defence barristers accused him of 'coaching' Safiya and urged the judge to throw the case out because he had disrupted their chance of a fair trial.

Before we knew it, our intermediary was in the witness box himself, trying to stay collected under tough, rigorous questioning. For a moment I feared the worst. It was certainly a grey area and it would be a marginal call. To our great relief, however, the judge ruled that the intermediary had acted properly, meaning that the trial could proceed.

After that, it was the defendants' turn to take to the witness box. They were weak under questioning and anyone would have struggled to convince a jury that it was normal to keep a young girl locked away in a cellar. Yet even though we had a confident case, I still couldn't relax. Now I was worried about the effect the length of the trial was having on the jury. Members kept leaving because of their work commitments or health, and the longer the trial went on, the more anxious I became. Soon we were down to nine jury members, the minimum number permitted. If we were to lose any more, we would be facing a retrial. I knew we couldn't afford to start again. I found myself jumping at every cough or sniffle, nervously scanning the faces of jurors, searching for any signs of poor health.

This time, my worries came to nothing: because finally, almost unbelievably, the trial was over. The remaining jurors had made it to the end unscathed. They reached a unanimous verdict, with the jury finding Safiya's captors Ilyas Ashar and Tallat Ashar guilty. After six months of torturous deliberations, relief flooded through me. I had prosecuted thousands of cases by this time, and I rarely let emotion get the better of me when the verdict was announced. I was often already thinking of what needed to be done next. But this was different, and the satisfaction was overwhelming. Safiya's case affected me deeply. I knew of the early awkward discussions she'd had with police when she had struggled to understand the concept of justice. It had immediately struck a chord with me, taking me back to my childhood when I'd grappled with the same problem. 'What is justice? What are the police?' she'd asked through sign language, after months spent teaching her to communicate.

In the courtroom, two female jurors were crying and Judge Lakin was speaking.

'You did not treat this girl as a human being,' he said, addressing Safiya's captors, Ilyas Ashar and his wife Tallat Ashar. 'To you she was merely an object to be used, abused and cast aside at will.' In October 2013, they were jailed for thirteen and five years respectively for rape, trafficking and furnishing false information to obtain a benefit. In 2014, their jail sentences were extended by the Court of Appeal.

What had started as a living hell for Safiya in a Salford cellar thirteen years earlier was finally over. She had confronted her traumas, was able to communicate and we had the convictions we wanted. But we hadn't finished yet.

Outside the court I conferred with my team. We still had work to do.

'I want to use the Proceeds of Crime Act to get their house,' I said. I wanted them to pay more than their meta-phorical dues.

'How are we going to do that?' asked a colleague, before reminding me that this kind of legislation had never been applied to traffickers before. It was an Act usually used to con-fiscate the houses of drug dealers.

I had been thinking about this idea for a while. 'We can prove they have financially benefitted from their crime,' I said. 'Aside from the benefit fraud, they used her for every-thing. She was an asset to them and she never received any money.' This was something we all agreed on. The next step, then, was to estimate what she might have earned had she not been a slave in a cellar.

I believed that we had enough evidence to make an applica-tion for their assets to be confiscated and that while our argument was unusual, it was also persuasive. And so it proved. In 2014, Manchester Crown Court ruled that the Ashars had to pay £321,000 towards the cost of their trials, and that Safiya would get £100,000 in compensation. The money from their confiscated assets in no way made up for what she'd suffered, but it could help towards her recovery and give her a chance to move on.

Safiya's case provoked widespread revulsion across the coun-try. But in truth, trafficking cases were beginning to make headlines on a frequent basis. In one case, a slavery ring that had seen twenty-four people held in appalling conditions at a travellers' camp was busted in Bedfordshire. In another, three women had been held captive in a South London house for thirty years. The Archbishop of Canterbury and the Pope no less were denouncing this 'grave evil' and the UK Human Trafficking Centre confirmed they had received almost 1,500 reports of suspected trafficking. This pushed politicians into action, and a draft Modern Slavery Bill was now circulating in the Commons. I watched the then-MP Frank Field speak eloquently in Parliament on how today's challenge compared to that faced by William Wilberforce 200 years previously.

'The shackles are different today,' he argued. 'There are no manacles; the slaves are not in irons. They are controlled even more effectively. Now the chains take a different form, and people do not believe such evil takes place.'

During the tabling of the Bill, I was invited to a government roundtable discussion on crime. I took the opportunity to raise Safiya's case with the Home Secretary Theresa May. Her countenance betrayed no emotion as I explained why we desperately needed a change in the law, that there had been no dedicated anti-trafficking legislation in almost two centuries. The National Crime Agency was about to be established, and there was a lot of talk about making slavery and trafficking a priority there. But this rhetoric needed to be accompanied by action. May nodded and held my gaze as I described Safiya's case, hoping to use her story to explain why we needed to guarantee victims more support and introduce tougher sentences.

I had heard promises from politicians before, and so was sceptical when she promised to treat this as a priority. But, as the sponsor of the Modern Slavery Act, May kept her word. In March 2015, the Bill gained Royal Assent and became law, introducing a modern slavery commissioner and an increase in the maximum custodial sentences for offenders from fourteen years to life. We couldn't have made such progress without the bravery and courage of Safiya and to this day I continue to be inspired by her.

Justice is never guaranteed. There's no inevitability that criminals face their day of reckoning. It only happens when people are prepared to take a stand. And for the most vulnerable this can be extremely hard. It makes achieving justice painfully difficult.

Around the same time as Safiya's case, I'd prosecuted a sexual abuse case against Michael Brewer, a choirmaster at Chetham's School of Music in Manchester. The key witness Frances Andrade found the ordeal of re-living her abuse too much and had taken her own life only days after giving evidence against her abuser. This had devastated me, as people said we – through the stress of the trial – had killed her. I only regained my sanity when I met her family who told me Frances had been self-harming ever since her abuse. Nonetheless, it was a tragic reminder of the enormous stresses placed on victims.

*

In the months and years that passed after Safiya's trial, I thought about her from time to time as I walked my dog along the canal. She had already made phenomenal progress from the petrified, tiny girl in the cellar to an assured young woman who was slowly taking control of her life. But I wondered where that life was taking her now.

One day I got my answer, when a colleague called to update me on her progress. For a few minutes I listened, utterly transfixed, and after the call I smiled and inhaled deeply, breathing in the scent of rain reawakening dry soil on the banks of the canal. Just for a moment, I broke into joyous laughter. I didn't think it was possible for Safiya to inspire me any more than she already had. As usual, though, she had exceeded all expectations.

In a crowded university theatre somewhere in Britain, hundreds of students were sliding into their seats, taking notebooks from their bags and waiting for their lecture to start. Among those climbing the steps to their seat was Safiya, who smiled as she introduced herself to the sign language interpreter, before sitting and eagerly taking notes. It was a scene that none of us imagined was possible when we first met her and was a wonderful next step on the remarkable journey she'd been on.

Safiya was making up for lost time. She was studying for a career in the NHS and moving from being cared for to caring for others. In some ways, the news didn't surprise me. Experiencing trust and support for the first time can have a genuinely transformative effect on people. I have no doubt whatsoever that it will only be a matter of time before she is dressed in hospital scrubs, working the wards and tending to others' needs, with whoever is fortunate enough to be treated by her placed in the most capable of hands. Safiya will always be the truest proof to me of just how powerful the human spirit can be.

XI

When we first arrived in Manchester, I told my family I would need time to get settled in. It would be a busy period, I warned them, and I had to get off to a good start. It would take at least six months to establish myself, I thought. But it wouldn't be long before we'd be able to enjoy a normal life, I promised them. Things would calm down soon enough, and I could correct the work – life balance that had been so out of kilter in London. Of course, the reality of things was entirely different. Those first few years in Manchester were a whirlwind of high-profile, high-stakes cases that not only made front-page news in the UK but also attracted international headlines.

When part of the BBC relocated to its new Salford home Media City in 2011, some argued that Auntie should move her sports coverage lock, stock and barrel to the north. Later on, it was also suggested – only half-jokingly – that perhaps all crime correspondents should move to Salford too. I could see why. From grooming gangs to drugs and gang killings, many of the country's biggest crimes were happening every day on the doorstep of my new home. Nevertheless, the work was invigorating, not least because my colleagues continued to demonstrate what made their office so different to my former one in London: the whole team was open to new ideas, allowing a more lateral approach to our work.

In those early days, I was at a senior management meeting at headquarters in East Manchester. We were surveying a list of force priorities for the year ahead, analysts clicking through a PowerPoint presentation as we watched. The screen showed the list:

1. Serious organised crime
2. Terrorism
3. Homicide
4. Serious violence
5. Domestic violence and sexual abuse

The discussion around the table turned to known criminals and gangs that the police were already targeting, and how dealing with them might help to address our priorities. I listened patiently and, when my turn came to speak, I asked if I could share some thoughts. In my experience, I said, they could deal with the top three priorities by focusing on violence against women and girls.

'There is a lot of research showing that people involved in organised crime and terrorism will also be violent towards their partners and the women and girls in their family,'

I explained. 'There's more than one way to disrupt criminal activity,' I added, thinking of Al Capone and his eventual imprisonment for tax offences much less high-octane than his other crimes. I told them about a case I had worked on previously in East London, investigating an Asian gang that MI5 had been monitoring. They were suspected of plotting terrorist activity, and so they were put under surveillance accordingly. However, there remained insufficient evidence to charge them. Covert recordings of them talking about how much they hated the UK, and how they planned to do something about it, wasn't enough. It was just talk, and talk alone didn't cross the evidence threshold for arrests to be made, particularly as the Metropolitan Police had become more risk averse on such matters, following some fatal mis-calculations. Jean Charles de Menezes, shot and killed at Stockwell tube station after being wrongly suspected of ter-rorism, when he was in fact an electrician with no criminal connections whatsoever, was one example. Such incidents had seriously damaged their reputation.

I understood the value of caution, but when we listened back to tapes of the gang's conversations, it was very clear that several of them had raped and violently abused women. In fact, they boasted openly about it. If the police could identify the victims and get them to come forward, then these men could be charged with sexual offences, getting them off the streets for a significant period of time. The Met agreed with this approach, and were able to find the victims and obtain the necessary evidence. Half a dozen men were subsequently charged with, and convicted for, rape. They all received significant sentences – eight to twelve years in prison each – and a potential terrorist cell was disrupted in the process. As I told this story, I could see heads nodding around the room.

'So why don't you shift number five, and make that your number one priority instead?'

This, it seemed, was a bridge too far.

'We can't do that,' said one officer. 'Serious organised crime and terrorism have to be our top priorities. They're set by government.'

'Fine. Put it at number three,' I responded. 'But think of it as one or two.' Everyone would be a winner: criminals off the street, their organised networks disrupted in the process.

There were murmurs of approval around the table, and the attendees agreed to adopt this mindset. I couldn't quite believe it. In Manchester, decisions were made much more quickly than in London's overcrowded bureaucracy.

If I had been sitting in a meeting with the Met senior management team making the same argument, I would have still been there eight years later trying to persuade them. Everything had to pass along a lengthy chain of command and be considered with excruciating care, meaning that change had an awfully long gestation period. Whereas here, I had just seen senior officers bypass this process and make a decision there and then. The pragmatism was thrilling.

They did things differently here, and I found the can-do culture hugely motivating, even energising. From the first day, I had the opportunity to develop new approaches. I was 200 miles away from CPS headquarters and all the government agencies and I could feel it: for the first time in years I was experiencing a real sense of freedom. Sometimes in my old post I had felt I needed to ask for permission to think. Here, I could just get on with the job. Rather than sounding people out when we wanted to do something in the Manchester office, I would simply email London and tell them I had done it. It was incredibly liberating.

Equally inspiring in Manchester was the fact I could see Peelian principles embodied in police leadership across the region. No one epitomised this more to me than Peter Fahy, Chief Constable in Manchester. Robert Peel is considered the father of modern policing and he was born just up the road in Bury. Among his nine principles of law enforcement, written in 1829, is the idea that the police needed the willing co-operation of the public. 'The police are the public and the public are the police,' said Peel, and the only difference between the two is that the police are paid to do their job, but we should all be working together for a just and fair society. Fahy intrinsically understood this.

He had taken over Greater Manchester Police at a difficult time, after his predecessor Michael Todd had been found dead on Mount Snowden. But it didn't take long for him to make his mark. He had a good instinct for what was happening in local communities and was always prepared to make sure that the public knew the police were on their side. When Sophie Lancaster was kicked to death in a mindless attack just because she was a goth, for example, Greater Manchester Police became the first force to start recording attacks on members of subcultures, including goths, punks and emos, as hate crimes. Although the legal definition of hate crime didn't traditionally include people like Sophie, Fahy made clear to people living alternative lifestyles that *his force* would include them under this definition. It was an inspired and intelligent move, and one that made people in the community feel a lot safer.

It was obvious to me that he had an enormous sense of public duty, and saw the public as his masters. Like me, he also knew that many people felt alienated by the justice system and was determined to transform the approach of his force, taking it from an institution with an obsession with property crime, league tables and targets to one that put the protection of vulnerable people at the heart of the police's work.

But still, some marginalised groups in the area had good reason to distrust the police. There were plenty of people in Manchester who could remember the former Chief Constable, James Anderton, who in 1986 had accused the gay community of 'swirling in a cesspit of their own making'.

To combat this mistrust, Fahy also made sure the police were active in local communities, supporting everything from boxing clubs and community allotments to dementia watch and youth football. I knew that prosecutors had to get into the fabric of local communities as well, and I intended to be a highly visible leader and raise the profile of prosecutors in the region. Knowing that Peter shared my priorities, I felt confident that we could achieve this. Every week I travelled to towns like Burnley, Carlisle and Blackburn, meeting gypsy and traveller groups, the LGBTQI+ community, local business people, Muslim groups, NHS Trusts, the Fire Service and the orthodox Jewish community. All of them told me the same thing. They had never met a prosecutor before. Our conversations only strengthened my beliefs that gaining, and maintaining, the public trust is the real way to reduce crime rates.

But maintaining confidence was often easier said than done. In a twenty-four-hour rolling news culture with the media wanting answers all the time, public trust was something you couldn't take for granted. It needed earning every day and therefore could disappear overnight. When communities felt threatened and ignored, that precious commodity could easily slip away – and this could create chaos. In one of my early cases in Manchester in 2011, I would experience this first hand.

It began with a report that found unexplained deaths in Stepping Hill Hospital, Stockport, along with severe and unexplained allergic reactions. The causes could not be pinpointed and, unsurprisingly, public anxiety was rising. Patients were discharging themselves against medical advice, staff were questioning each other – and naturally media interest in the situation was growing.

As soon as the first post-mortem result arrived, confirming the diagnosis of the other living victims, we knew immediately that we were in criminal territory. The evidence suggested that someone was tampering with the saline drips, loading them with insulin to put patients into hypoglycaemic shock, which could have fatal consequences – and indeed already had.

The hospital was big, though, and full of people coming and going. It was like a Poirot mystery, but one with seven hundred suspects. At that point, we couldn't even properly establish who had been at the scene of the crimes. The pharmacy where the insulin and saline drips were stored was not secure and could be accessed by staff in the course of their work, as well by anyone with more malign intentions. Meanwhile, people were dying. Five patients would be killed, and another left permanently brain damaged. Comparisons were already being made with Harold Shipman, the serial killer GP.

The police inquiry tried to isolate the killer or killers: the doctors, nurses and other staff members were no longer permitted to work alone, so that all activity could be monitored. Or could it be a patient? Or even a visitor?

There were over a hundred officers on the case, as well as almost every forensic team and every medical expert in the area, despite the fact we had hundreds of other serious cases to deal with. We knew exactly how grave the consequences could be if the killer wasn't found, not just because of the loss of life but because of the loss of faith in what should have been a safe, healing place.

Then one of my prosecutors received a call from Detective Superintendent Simon Barraclough, the senior investigating officer. He suggested that they might have made a break-through and that a nurse, Rebecca Leighton, was of special interest to the inquiry. But the evidence against Leighton wasn't strong, and I had doubts as to whether it was right to charge her. Yes, she worked on the wards in question and had been on duty at the exact time the contamination was thought to have taken place. She had also stolen some prescribed medicine from the hospital pharmacy. Yet there was little else to connect her to these murders.

Compromising, I gave authority to charge her, but not for murder or grievous bodily harm, because we couldn't show that she injected the insulin into the bags. Of course, the media immediately assumed she was the poisoner. We didn't correct their assumption, because we just didn't know enough.

Leighton was remanded in custody while inquiries continued. We were all concerned that the evidence we had expected – forensics, fingerprints from saline dips – was coming back from the lab with nothing to connect Leighton to the crimes. Examining CCTV, there was nothing unusual about her behaviour, and neither witnesses nor fellow staff members had anything incriminating to say about her. The only thing we could prove was that she had medication at home that had been taken from the hospital, which is theft.

Days became weeks, and the police were increasingly disheartened by the lack of evidence. I sat down with the CPS lawyer and DS Barraclough and we went through what we had. It was clear that Leighton was guilty of nothing beyond the theft, and she should not stay in prison any longer. We discontinued the case against her, and she was released. Then I sat down and set to work at my least favourite task: writing a press release.

I still regret the speed with which we wrongly charged Leighton, but it reminded me that the strength of public scrutiny, while entirely justified, could also create a pressure cooker in which mistakes could be, and were, made. I am truly sorry to Rebecca Leighton for suspecting her of murder. She rightly obtained damages for her wrongful imprisonment.

The police inquiry continued quietly. There was a new lead: a Filipino-trained nurse called Victorino Chua. He wasn't particularly well-liked at the hospital and, as we later learned most definitively, the feeling was mutual. He came to the attention of the investigation one morning, after the discovery that the medical charts of some patients were deliberately altered, so that the patients in question would have been given inaccurate, possibly fatal, doses of medication. The finger of suspicion pointed squarely at Chua. He had been on duty at the right time, but he had also been involved in a public row the night before with the daughter of one of the patients, causing her to leave the hospital in tears.

After further investigation, we found that Chua might have a connection to the other crimes. Now we had Chua with the opportunity and the means. Possibly also the motive: he seemed to dislike his job and often argued with his fellow staff and patients, who had a low opinion of him. But did that make him a killer? The evidence was strong enough for us to make an arrest and we were able to search his home (which once again attracted the attention of the press . . .). This time it was the right call: police discovered a thirteen-page confessional letter in a kitchen drawer.

It was chilling stuff. Chua called his letter 'the bitter nurse confession' and described himself as 'an angel turned into an evil person' who would 'go straight to hell'. He spoke of his hatred of some of the staff at the hospital and admitted 'there is a devil in me'. He didn't actually admit to committing the crime, however. The police were convinced there was enough evidence now to charge him with murder, manslaughter and some offences involving the tampering of drips. I couldn't help but think of the court clock, however, ticking away: our evidence wasn't yet strong enough to take to trial and if we didn't get it right, Chua would walk free.

In cases like this, accompanied by genuine public panic, it is necessary to act at speed to quell the unrest, but decisions still – always – need to be executed with meticulous precision, as there is little margin for error. We'd got it wrong with Rebecca Leighton and I certainly didn't want to do the same again. At that moment, this case rested entirely on medical and scientific evidence that was circumstantial in nature and therefore couldn't be put before a jury. If we tried to do so, the judge would rightly dismiss the case. And if Chua was charged, then he would have to be kept in custody until the conclusion of his trial and there was no way we could be ready for that trial within a year, given the evidence still to collect. He couldn't be kept in custody pending trial for that long; the judge would give us a timetable for trial that we couldn't realistically meet, and Chua would be freed. It was finally agreed that releasing him on strict bail conditions was the right approach. Chua could hurt nobody else at the hospital, nor could he leave the country.

Ultimately, it was the right choice. It would take the best part of eighteen months to gather sufficient evidence to place Chua in the room with the tampered drip. We interviewed nearly 1,200 people and eliminated hundreds of other potential suspects along the way, until only Chua remained. It was vital that we got it right, because the trial was becoming expensive.

The public rarely view the cost of an investigation and prosecution in financial terms. But as taxpayers, the truth is that it's their money we're spending in each case. On average, it costs £1 million to investigate and prosecute a single murder. That covers a lot of staffing costs: police officers, prosecutors, barristers, as well as the administration and preparation of paperwork, the collection of evidence and the forensic work that has to be done. A great deal of expertise is required, and that doesn't come cheap.

The Stepping Hill poisoner case exceeded that cost considerably. By several million pounds, in fact. This was necessary because of the unique complications of the case: it became an unusually public inquiry into the failings of a hospital that were not untypical in the country at the time. We needed to challenge the poor security, the easy access to insecure areas, the poor logging of drugs, the inadequate timekeeping records and use of CCTV, the lack of staff supervision. The case had also exposed a flaw in the procedures for recruiting staff from overseas.

Chua had studied and trained in the Philippines and come to the UK to practise as a nurse because we don't train enough health professionals here to meet our needs. We get around this by regularly raiding other countries, to take their hard-earned nurses and doctors to fill the thousands of vacant positions in our own hospitals. The Philippines and India accounted for the largest number of foreign nurses working in England, and these practitioners are almost invariably excellent: hard-working and an invaluable asset to our NHS. It wouldn't function without them. However, in building the case against Chua, the police looked into his qualifications, and became concerned that he might never have actually obtained them. There were loopholes in the system, and Chua may well have exploited them. I passed this information on to the Department of Health, suggesting that their systems for checking staff might need to become more robust. They ordered a National Inquiry, made by the Nursing and Midwifery Council, which delivered several recommendations that ultimately saw sweeping changes introduced. Hospitals altered their security procedures and the government invested in a raft of new procedures, including a clinical test of competence, along with a more robust system of face-to-face identity checks and advanced passport scanning technology to verify identity documents, meaning the public could continue to be assured of the safety of their hospitals.

Chua was eventually found guilty of thirty-three charges: two counts of murder, twenty-two counts of attempting to cause grievous bodily harm, one of causing grievous bodily harm, seven of attempting to administer a poison and one of administering a poison. He received twenty-five life sentences and was jailed for a minimum of thirty-five years.

That summer, public confidence in the police sank even lower. On 4 August 2011, the Metropolitan Police shot and killed a man named Mark Duggan in Tottenham, North London, suspecting him of being in possession of a handgun. The authorities initially reported that Duggan was shot in an exchange of fire, but this was soon proved to be false. Trust between the police and locals in the area was already poor, and had been there for years – the black community often had a difficult relationship with the police. I couldn't help but sympathise with the community, as they had undeniable reasons for their feelings: from the institutional racism that had been proven to run through the force in the Stephen Lawrence case, through to discriminatory practices such as stop and search, which disproportionately targeted the black community. For decades, these simmering tensions were ignored, but more than once they had boiled over.

In January 1981, thirteen young black people died in a house fire that locals suspected was not an accident. They also believed that the police were failing to investigate properly and a march was organised in protest, known as the Black People's Day of Action. A month later, with robbery and violent crime on the increase in Brixton, the Metropolitan Police introduced Operation Swamp, an oppressive stop and search exercise, which saw nearly 1,000 people stopped, with 82 arrested over five days. It was enough to ensure the already tense relationship between police and locals finally came to a head. When a black youth named Michael Bailey was stabbed by criminals, police gathered as they awaited an ambulance. Fearing arrest, Bailey resisted police help and locals tried to intervene, fearing the worst.

This spark lit the fuse of the Brixton riots, one of the worst disorders on the streets of London that century. Lord Scarman's report for the government afterwards said there was 'no doubt racial disadvantage was a fact of current British life'.

Only a few years later, a black woman on the Broadwater council estate in Tottenham died of a heart attack after four police burst into her home, triggering some of the ugliest rioting in memory. A police officer was chased by a crowd, surrounded and stabbed to death, his colleague badly wounded. The fraught relations between the police and the black community continued to exist, and I couldn't help but wonder if we had missed an opportunity to learn some lessons.

After Mark Duggan was killed, people took to the streets. That same day a protest outside Tottenham police station quickly turned ugly. Demonstrators had been shouting 'we want answers' and, when none were forthcoming, two police cars were set on fire. Rioting began, and soon spread first to other parts of London, then out and beyond, to other parts of the country. Duggan was the nephew of the deceased Manchester gangster Desmond Noonan and police had been warned that a hardcore criminal element had spied an opportunity for orchestrated violence. While these riots might have supercifially been linked to Duggan's death, for some it was seized upon as an opportunity to cause chaos. So it didn't come as a surprise when crowds started to gather around Salford precinct – but the level of violence and criminality that followed shocked us all. This was no peaceful protest: it was a deliberate attempt to maim the police.

Thugs wearing hoods and bandanas launched a barrage of missiles, including bricks, breezeblocks, scaffolding poles, concrete slabs and stones at officers, who held up riot shields and tried to hold their ground. Some sustained head injuries and fell to the ground, dropping their shields in the process. They were incredibly vulnerable. The police were vastly outnumbered, and the number of injuries was growing. Over a thousand people were now part of the rioting group: as one officer later said, 'the sky just went black due to the sheer number of missiles in the air'. Cars were overturned and torched, including one belonging to the BBC. As the violence spread, windows were smashed, shops set alight, and firefighters and journalists were also attacked. The sheer brutality forced the police to withdraw and call for help from neighbouring forces. Officers would later tell researchers that they feared they would be killed that day. Meanwhile, the violence continued to spill out into the community. The local shopping centre, a Lidl supermarket and an off-licence were all ransacked. The city was burning and residents were terrified as forces struggled to get the situation under control.

But the police now had another battle on their hands. Where were they going to put the people they were arresting? They were rapidly running out of cell space, with prisoners now being kept in vans outside stations for lack of better options. We were losing control.

I decided that we would need to open the courts to deal with the overflow and make sure justice was delivered swiftly. My staff agreed to work through the night, and we brought together enough court staff, prosecutors and defence lawyers to make the plan workable. We would keep the courts open all night. We worked quickly, reviewing the cases as the police gathered the paperwork and witness statements in order to process the offenders quickly.

I thought carefully about the best way to bring some order to the situation. Those convicted of low-level public order offences would come first. These were people who had caused criminal damage or abused police officers. Most of them pleaded guilty, so it was fairly easy to get the cases through the courts with relative speed, using the Police National Computer system to check for previous offences in similar areas. Our job was to empty the cells in order to safely house the more serious offenders. Meanwhile, in London, where the riots had started three days earlier, the authorities were still considering even whether to establish a night court. It was another reminder of how we were able to get things done more quickly in Manchester.

Over 100 people were brought before the court that evening, and we finished for the night around 1am. The next morning, the police vans returned. This time, though, they were bringing the more serious offenders to court. The magistrates did not have sufficient powers to give these people a jail sentence, so they would have to commit them to the Crown Court for sentencing instead. This would normally take weeks, but the Recorder understood the gravity of the situation and agreed we could expedite some of these cases.

As we prepared each case, I thought about the riots, and how genuine protest could be commandeered by thuggery and devastation. I thought of the shopkeepers who had lost their livelihoods, their businesses now trashed or set on fire. I thought of the sixty police officers who had been injured as missiles rained down upon them. I thought of what it must have been like standing behind a police shield as an angry mob surged forward. And I thought of my own children sitting at home listening to police helicopters circling over-head and watching the news. 'Dad, I'm scared,' my son had told me. 'When is it going to stop?' I wanted to make clear in the prosecution of these cases that they were crimes against the community, and indeed were crimes that often destroyed communities. It reminded me of my brother, trying to make his own shop more secure after endless robberies. How, I wondered, could the fear in the communities be conveyed?

I put down the case summary in my hand and looked up at my team.

'When we're prosecuting these people, it's not enough just to think they're guilty of theft, damaging public property or whatever,' I said. 'Surely the circumstances in which they carry out these crimes are relevant too?'

They knew immediately what I was driving at. Every criminal act, no matter how minor, fuelled the lawless chaos. They were all part of a bigger crime. But how would we get this across to the judge?

I immediately thought of 'Community Impact Statements', which had been introduced in 2006 and allowed community groups to advise the judge on the effect a type of crime was having on their area. The idea had come from US-style community courts, but it never took off in the UK. Ironically, they were piloted at the Salford court, but had never been used since. This could be the moment to put them properly to use.

In the remaining hours of the afternoon, the police and local authorities composed a statement together, to reflect their recent experiences of engagement within the community. Many of them, they revealed, had long felt frightened in their own homes and certainly didn't feel able to socialise in the area; they felt that their lives could be at risk. That feeling of threat, I knew, could destroy lives. The statements were served on every defence lawyer due to appear at court. I advised the prosecution counsel to refer to the Community Impact Statements when sentencing and, when the defendants appeared in court the following morning, the judge made it clear he was significantly increasing sentences as a result. The message to them was clear: their jail terms had been increased because of the fear and anxiety that their crimes had created in the community. This meant the public could feel assured: the law's job was to keep them safe.

An eighteen-year-old who admitted burglary in Sainsbury's was sentenced to two years in a young offenders' institution. Another man who was caught with a bag of stolen clothes was jailed for sixteen months. The man who lit the match that set fire to the BBC car was sentenced to five and a half years' imprisonment. And another young man who wandered into Patisserie Valerie while it was being looted and stole an ice cream was jailed for sixteen months. The sentences were considerably higher than what offenders would normally receive for such crimes.

Not everyone thought this approach was the best one. But those people talking about sentencing guidelines and judges being disproportionate weren't there, and weren't affected by the full force of the crimes in question. They didn't live in the places that had been trashed by criminals and they didn't understand the damage that had been done to our communities. In contrast, I wanted the judge to be aware not only of the behaviour of individuals in isolation but of the full background and its impact on the community. I felt it was proportionate sentencing based on the context in which a crime takes place.

When I think back, I shudder to think what might have happened if those riots had taken place just a few years later, when cuts to police and the justice system by the coalition government had begun to be felt. By 2015 we had 25 per cent fewer prosecutors and Greater Manchester Police had lost nearly 2,000 police officers and 1,000 police staff as a result of budget cuts. Youth workers, who worked tirelessly to warn young people of the consequences of getting involved in crime and help them find a better path, had seen their services decimated. In fact, youth services had all but disappeared. Ten police stations in Greater Manchester alone had closed; across England and Wales half of all Magistrates' Courts had closed. It makes for sobering reading, especially because these cuts are often felt most keenly by the most vulnerable communities, where criminal behaviour can be seen as a way out of poverty. It becomes a vicious cycle.

Public perception of crime is probably as accurate a measure of the police's successes as actual crime statistics – and public fear of crime has remained stubbornly high. In 2011, for example, despite crime levels supposedly falling to their lowest levels in thirty years, the British Crime Survey showed that 60 per cent of adults aged sixteen and over thought crime was rising.

Ours is an age of insecurity, the flames fanned by the media, and a diminishing presence of justice on the streets only makes this problem worse, particularly when combined with increasing job insecurity and rising levels of poverty.

In the summer of 2011, the anxiety and uncertainty in our communities were already tangible. In both of these cases I had seen the results: the fear of going into hospital in Chua's case and widespread panic caused by violent disorder on the streets of our cities. But now I was to be faced by an even more fundamental fear: that of people being attacked in their own home.

Just before the riots, Greater Manchester Police had dealt with the case of Peter Flanagan. Confronted in his own home by machete-wielding intruders, in defending himself Flanagan had stabbed one – and killed him. He had subsequently been arrested and was now in custody.

The day before, the Prime Minister David Cameron had given a speech on why, in his view, homeowners needed the right to defend themselves. If their house had been broken into, he said, they should not be prosecuted. That intervention made sure this was going to be a politically sensitive case. I agreed with Cameron in this instance, and so was pleased when I heard that Flanagan had been bailed. In the wake of his arrest, there had been talk of new legislation needing to be introduced to clarify the law, but I was of the view that the law – for once! – was clear enough already. I just needed to be in full possession of the facts. I asked an officer to prepare a file on the case as speedily as possible and within three weeks I had a full file of evidence showing that Flanagan's version of events was correct and that he had acted in self-defence to protect his property. The law was clear enough here, I believed, to give him a full defence against the allegation of murder. I told the officer that he wouldn't be charged and no further action would be required. On my way out, the investigating officer asked if I wanted to write a press release.

'No,' I responded. 'I won't be issuing a press release.' Instead, I planned on speaking straight to the camera. In response to this case and to Cameron's statement, some politicians had been casting doubts on whether the law was on the side of homeowners who used reasonable force to protect their property. I needed to give the public full assurance that it was, and I said as much on the news that evening.

I hoped then that the matter would be put to bed. But four days later, there was another, similar, case. This time, Cecil Coley, an elderly shopkeeper in Manchester, had stabbed an armed robber in his shop. The seventy-two-year-old florist had been playing dominos with a friend after closing time when four armed men burst into his store and demanded the takings. The struggle that ensued concluded with one of the robbers collapsing on the pavement outside with a stab wound to his chest. He subsequently died. Once again, we decided that a man defending himself from violent intrusion would not be prosecuted for his act of self-defence.

But this crime seemed to follow me around: another incident of home invasion happened in South Manchester little more than a month later. This time, a burglar posing as a gas man broke into the home of Vincent Cooke and held him at knifepoint while demanding he open his safe. Cooke fought back and during the struggle, grabbed a knife from the kitchen and stabbed the burglar in self-defence, killing him in the process. As in the other two cases, I was able to clear Cooke of any charges, as he had acted honestly and instinctively to protect himself and his family from intruders.

Shortly afterwards, I believe someone raised these three cases with the Justice Secretary and, somewhat sarcastically, asked if he still believed the law needed clarification, when every time we had managed to protect the householder against the burglar. There wasn't a lot he could say.

Some crimes provoke a deep, atavistic reaction – and this was one such crime. Many would feel, with good reason, that if you can't protect your home, your business and family, then what is the law for? The sanctity of the home can be traced right back to the days of early English common law. In Parliament in 1763, William Pitt (the Elder) said that 'the poorest man may in his cottage bid defiance to all the forces of the Crown', and the sentiment had endured. Just think of the old adage: for an Englishman, his home is his castle.

Our job was always to act in service of the public. While

commentators might complain in some instances that sentencing was too harsh in some cases, or in other instances that prosecutions should have been made when they weren't, everything we did sought to make sure that the public at large were safe from harm. More than that: the public should not just *be* safe, they should *feel* safe. It sounds straightforward, but is very difficult to achieve.

To give the public assurance, build confidence and convince people the law was on their side were all crucial. But it was becoming more difficult. People were losing trust in institutions: the police, the church, the banks, business, Parliament and the media were all at risk of losing public respect.

Plenty of people in my profession were in denial about this. They believed the hallowed institution of justice would always endure and that the justice system itself would stand apart from caprices and passing fads. In my view, this was a dangerous kind of institutional blind faith, and if we didn't take action to regain that trust, there would be serious consequences, both in the justice system and in wider society. The idea of involving the community in my work had always been a core belief of mine, and each case I dealt with only strengthened this: if the public didn't know we were there, if they didn't know what we were doing and why, then what was the point? As a prosecutor, I needed to be more of an activist, not just another bureaucrat.

XII

Kiaran Stapleton sat alone, toying with his food. Several minutes passed as he stared straight ahead, his fork never quite reaching his mouth. He bristled with nervous energy in the dimly lit restaurant. Occasionally he would get up from his seat and pace the floor, peering out of the windows of the Campanile hotel at the passing traffic on Regent Road. It could have been a scene from an Edward Hopper painting. But this was not a study of urban isolation, nor a noirish exploration of melancholy. This was a CCTV portrait of a violent sociopath.

Stapleton betrayed little emotion as he watched the police beyond the windows begin their investigation on the streets of Salford. Police tape was strung up across the pavement and forensic officers were searching for evidence. Stapleton had booked into the hotel earlier and had been waiting all afternoon for this moment. Now it was showtime.

I was beginning my third decade as a prosecutor and after such a long time on the job it could be easy to slip into complacency. Instead, the previous six months had been remarkably invigorating, providing me with enormous scope to learn – including opportunities to redraw the judicial map, which I had seized with both hands. I had always been conscious of the wider consequences of any decisions I made, but the realisation of the bigger impact of every crime and every judgment had sharpened over time, and continued to stay at the forefront of my mind. It was Christmas, and I was taking a rare few days with my family. On Boxing Day, the phone rang.

'There's been a shooting,' said the voice on the other end of the line.

So much for the festive season.

It was 2011. Anuj Bidve had his whole life ahead of him when he set off from his hotel with a group of friends to the Boxing Day sales in Manchester. He was a twenty-three-year-old international student from India studying for a Master of Science degree in Microelectronics and System-on-Chip Engineering at Lancaster University. His parents had borrowed £30,000 to help their only son study in England and Anuj was planning to return to his home in Pune as soon as he had completed his studies. His father later said he carried with him the hopes and dreams of the family. Until he met Kiaran Stapleton.

Early that morning, Stapleton crossed the road and asked Anuj and his friends for the time. When Anuj told him it was 1.30am, Stapleton reached into his pocket and turned to face him. Producing a 9mm Glock handgun, Stapleton raised the gun to Anuj's temple and pulled the trigger. Then he ran off laughing. The killing was completely unprovoked: a random, motiveless murder that would send shockwaves far beyond the UK.

As I took the call at home, camera crews were already congregating at the scene. Meanwhile, armed police were stopping and searching youths on the Ordsall estate, fully aware of the fear ethnic minorities in the area must be feeling while the culprit was still at large: after all, it could very well be a hate crime. The Indian government had already moved quickly to seek assurances that Indian students were safe in Britain, and in the next few days David Cameron called the victim's family, who had been flown in by Greater Manchester Police, to promise them that justice would be delivered. Some crimes have international implications, and this was one of them. There were almost 40,000 Indian students in the UK, many of whom would stay on and do vital work for Britain's economy. If they were to decide that Britain was too dangerous a place for them, as had happened elsewhere, then we would definitely feel the loss. Anuj's father Subhash told journalists he expected the number of Indian students studying in the UK would be 'reduced drastically' the following year, and he was proven correct. Within a year, there would be almost 20,000 fewer Indian students – and that number would continue to fall. By 2015, there were little more than 15,000 Indian students in the UK.

I had long seen victims of crimes as representative of a whole community of victims. The victims in Rochdale represented all ignored and neglected children. And, to me, Anuj represented the children of all parents who wanted their child to have the opportunities that they had never had. It felt personal, because I was one of those same children. Christmas was suddenly the last thing on my mind.

How would we find this perpetrator? Winning confidence and gaining information from tight-knit communities like Ordsall was a real challenge for the police. Some would say it was almost impossible. This was, after all, home to the notorious crime boss known as 'Mr Big', Paul Massey.

Massey cast a long shadow over the area and made community relations with police difficult, to say the least. To 'grass' someone on Massey's patch was often seen as a worse offence than the original crime. Nevertheless, Greater Manchester Police had managed to glean sufficient intelligence to identify a suspect in Kiaran Stapleton, an angry young man who was known for random acts of aggression. He had previous convictions (he was in fact on bail over a road-rage attack at the time) and connections with another crime family, the Noonans. Stapleton's aunt had married the gangland boss Damian Noonan and Stapleton aspired to have the same gangster status. The seemingly random murder he had carried out could well have been a gang initiation ritual to prove his right to belong in criminal company.

Shortly afterwards, Stapleton was arrested at a house in Leigh, where he was hiding out. Now the clock was ticking, and we needed to find a way to charge him but, as so often in the immediate aftermath of a crime, the evidence we had was not very strong. We knew Stapleton had booked himself into the Campanile hotel the day after the murder, and that he had been watching the police at the crime scene. We also knew that in the last few days, he'd had tattooed beneath his eye a teardrop, a tattoo that often indicates its bearer has committed murder. Still, this wasn't enough to stand as evidence and without more, we would have to release him in thirty-six hours.

However, Stapleton had not acted alone. He had an accomplice, a man who had been at his side as he ran away laughing. Ryan Holden. It was during interviews that we realised Ryan wasn't quite cut from the same cloth as Kiaran. In fact, whereas Stapleton showed no remorse – nor much emotion at all – Ryan seemed genuinely upset. In an off-the-record conversation with police, he admitted to seeing Kiaran shoot Bidve but claimed that he hadn't known Kiaran's intentions beforehand. He said he felt sick at what had happened. Of course, given this was off the record, we couldn't use it in court: the question now was whether we could get Ryan to give evidence against Stapleton and in what circumstances. The police went off to speak to his solicitor, and an officer came back to me promptly and put their demands on the table.

'He wants to be given immunity from prosecution and a new identity,' the officer reported. If that was possible, then he might consider talking. I weighed this up. Ryan wasn't involved in the crime itself, and so immunity wasn't something I could consider in this case. But he was a witness, and we could provide him with protection as a result. The officer nodded in agreement, and headed off to relay our offer to Ryan and his solicitor.

By then, we only had a few hours remaining to keep Stapleton in custody, but Ryan came through: he gave a full interview, explaining in detail what happened that night. We now had impeccable evidence from a witness and I was able to give the police written authority that Stapleton should be charged with murder. I called the High Commission of India in London to explain this, and also to give them full assurances that this had not been a case of Indian students being targeted.

'This is not a hate crime,' I emphasised. 'It was gang related, and unfortunately Anuj was in the wrong place at the wrong time.' Stapleton had indeed wanted to raise his status in the local crime community.

A week later, he appeared in court for a plea and direction hearing. He entered a plea of guilty to manslaughter charges on the grounds of diminished responsibility. Stapleton, I could see, was loving the attention, and performing the role of an unhinged maniac. He wanted the court to believe his mental functions were impaired so he couldn't be fully liable for his actions. He even introduced himself to the judge as 'Psycho'. Needless to say, I wasn't falling for it. I told the prosecution team we wouldn't be accepting his defence and would go to trial. Not only that, we'd expedite it, given the international interest in the case. When I had spoken to the victim's parents to offer my condolences, they had told me how homicide cases could take the best part of a decade in India and, in many instances, no one was ever prosecuted. They were fearful that the same would happen here. I had assured them justice was delivered much more swiftly here and was able to keep my promise: the trial was set for four months later. Bidve's parents were flown over and they sat in court every day, watching the trial of the murderer of their son. Ryan was now in witness protection – as were his immediate family, including his cousin, who was the mother of Stapleton's child – so he gave evidence from behind a screen. When asked by the defence why he hadn't told the police about the actions of Stapleton before now, he replied that if he had done, he'd 'have been dead within a week'. It was a brutal reminder of how dangerous the honour codes of gangs could be.

When the jury came back from their deliberations I was in Manchester Crown Court, eagerly awaiting the verdict. Guilty. Bidve's parents were sitting just in front of me and, after the loud cheers that accompanied the verdict died down, they both turned to me. I offered my hand, not knowing what to say, and his mother grabbed and kissed it. Her gesture was just too much and I dissolved into tears. In fact, tears were flowing down everyone's cheeks. I tried to compose myself.

'I'm just doing my job,' I said. 'You don't have to thank me.'

She continued to thank me, and in the end I had to gently prise my hand away and head for the door. I passed several police officers and congratulated them on a great job and then rushed straight back to my office, locked the door and slumped in my chair, unable to control the tears.

I thought of my own parents and the sacrifices they had made so that I could have a better life. I couldn't remember ever having felt so vulnerable after the resolution of a case as I did now. At least I could take some comfort from the trial reports. Stapleton was jailed for life with a minimum of thirty years and we had delivered justice in just over six months. The Indian media, which had initially portrayed the UK as somewhere not safe for Indian students, were now praising us. They knew as well as we did that justice delayed often resulted in justice denied.

I would soon encounter another of the most notorious members of the dark criminal underworld of my new home city: Dale Cregan, a violent drug dealer with an interest in guns.

Cregan had been involved in petty crime in the area from a young age and, by the time he was twenty-two, he was said to be earning £20,000 a week from dealing cocaine. He was an emerging figure in the East Manchester criminal underworld and had a fearsome reputation. The fact he had lost an eye in a fight, and wore a false black onyx one in its place, only added to his menace.

By May 2012 he was one of Greater Manchester Police's most wanted criminals, having shot dead an amateur boxer called Mark Short in a pub in Droylsden, and attempted to kill three other men at the same time. The killing was part of a long-running dispute between two families – the Atkinsons and the Shorts – which had escalated from fights and knee-cappings to full-blown war.

We had clear intelligence that Cregan was responsible but, as usual, intelligence did not equal evidence. Despite the fact he wore a balaclava during the act itself, plenty of people knew that Cregan was behind the attack. However, even though the crime took place in a crowded pub, no one was willing to speak out. It was even less likely that anyone would give evidence in a courtroom, even with the offer of witness protection. He was simply too dangerous, too powerful. This meant that even though Cregan had been arrested by police at Manchester Airport, we had to release him on bail. I was immensely frustrated. We just didn't have enough evidence to charge him with murder.

Knowing the police were on to him did little to deter Cregan, however, and he only had one thing in mind: resuming his feud with the Short family. Anticipating their retaliation, he wanted to send out an unequivocal message to his enemies before they got to him. Through a tip-off, the police found out that he was plotting to kill David Short.

They moved quickly to bring him in for questioning but when they reached his home, Cregan wasn't there. He had already fled.

No one had any idea where he was until a few days later, when Short's murder was reported. He was at home, and Cregan had shot him nine times, before throwing a grenade and blowing his body apart. It was astonishingly brutal. This was the first time a grenade had been used as a murder weapon in mainland Britain, and Cregan clearly felt the thrill: he threw a second ten minutes later at a nearby house. This one didn't kill anyone, but Cregan had miscalculated: he was caught on CCTV in the process. We now had the evidence we needed to charge him.

'You've got enough,' I told the senior investigating officer. 'Go get him.'

That, of course was easier said than done. Cregan was now being moved round the country by his accomplices and would remain on the run for over a month. Understandably, the media were fixated on the extraordinary story, and the police were struggling in the face of the wall of silence from the community. To combat it, a reward of £25,000 was suggested for information leading to his capture. It was nowhere near enough.

'Anyone who gives us information on where Cregan is wouldn't live long enough to spend it,' said the senior investigating officer. He felt the reward should be a million pounds. I agreed and so did other senior officers, including Peter Fahy.

If we offered that kind of reward, there was a good chance someone would come forward and betray Cregan. Yes, it was a large amount and an extreme measure. But the circumstances justified it.

The Home Office thought differently and blocked the idea straight away. They told us that crime shouldn't pay, and nor should witnesses of crimes be that richly rewarded either. The reward was set at £50,000. I knew such a sum would have little impact on the *omertà*. Indeed, Cregan's supporters responded straight away with their counter offer: posters appeared in Manchester announcing a £50,000 bounty, which would be offered to kill anyone who grassed on Dale Cregan.

Meanwhile, it seemed that he had disappeared. Police simply couldn't trace his communications. We would later learn that he was using Xbox to stay in touch with other gang members to maintain his cover. He continued to remain one step ahead of us, and his supporters were as determined as him that it would stay that way.

During that summer, over a hundred police warnings were issued to people in Manchester to let them know there was a real and immediate threat to their life, such was the size of the criminal network and the paranoia of Cregan's henchmen. I had never seen the like before, even when I had been in London. Police all over the country were now involved, working on a manhunt of unprecedented scale. We had started to have some success in picking off his associates and charging them, including people involved in the David Short murder, but Cregan himself remained elusive. However, his mother was now under twenty-four-hour surveillance, in the hope that she might provide a lead. It was this that would provoke him to commit his most horrifying crime to date.

He later said he was angry that his mum was being harassed, which was why he made a hoax call from his hideout in East Manchester to police on 18 September. Giving a false name, he claimed someone had thrown a concrete slab through his back window. He spoke for just over a minute to a call handler who confirmed that they'd send someone round within an hour to the address he'd given in Mottram in Longdendale.

'Thanks very much,' he responded. 'I'll be waiting.'

And so he was, as PCs Nicola Hughes and Fiona Bone set off in a marked VW transporter van. They were unarmed, except for Fiona's Taser, and unaware they were walking into a fatal ambush. The two officers were young; Nicola was twenty-three and Fiona thirty-two, and had less than a decade's experience in the police between them. Not that any experience would have prepared them for what happened as they walked through the small front garden to attend what they thought was a routine incident.

As they walked up the path, the door opened and Cregan appeared, firing a semi-automatic weapon straight at them. The first shots failed to penetrate their body armour but as they desperately tried to retreat, there was no escaping the hail of bullets. Cregan shot Nicola in the back, paralysing her immediately. She fell on to the path and was shot three more times as she lay immobile.

Seeing her colleague go down, Fiona reached for her Taser and stood her ground as Cregan turned his gun on her. She managed to draw and fire it, but only into the ground. As she did so, Cregan hit her with a bullet that penetrated the side of her body armour. The bullet hit her heart, and she died at the scene.

But Cregan hadn't finished yet. He walked over to Nicola and stood over her. Then he shot her several times in the head, until he'd completely emptied his extended magazine of 9mm cartridges. Before he fled the property in a stolen BMW, he pulled the pin on a military grenade and threw it back into the garden where both officers lay on the floor. Fiona and Nicola never had a chance of survival.

I received a call shortly afterwards to say the police had Cregan. I was astonished: he had walked into Hyde police station and confessed to the murders.

'I've murdered two police officers,' he told officers at the desk. 'You were hounding my family, so I took it out on yours.'

It transpired that Cregan had been staying in the home of a family that he had threatened, essentially holding them hostage so he could protect his cover. We would need to debrief them, and they would undoubtedly be traumatised. And we would need to interview Cregan himself. Everyone said he was mad, and his solicitor would of course be looking at a defence of diminished responsibility. We had to rule this out immediately, so that he could be properly punished. We knew he was in his right mind: he was simply a psychopath. I could have charged him in minutes with murder, but first we had to prove his mental state.

'Use all of the thirty-six hours we have to interview him,' I told an officer.

When a colleague is killed, the effect on the whole force is enormous. It is a tragedy when officers are killed trying to protect the public, and there is no way to ease the pain. Peter Fahy was utterly devastated at the loss of two of his officers.

'You cannot blame yourself for this, Peter,' I said down the phone. 'No one could have known what would happen.'

Peter was an exemplary leader, though, so couldn't help but feel the loss personally. He really did see the police as a family. At the swearing in of new recruits, Fahy would meet their parents, as the officers were formally attested. He saw the trepidation in their eyes, their fear for the safety of their loved ones. He knew their service would sometimes place them at risk. And so I knew he may well feel he had let down the families of Fiona and Nicola by failing to protect them. The next time I saw him, it was as though he had aged ten years.

It was the first time two British female officers had been killed together on duty, and the entire police force went into mourning. Many were traumatised by it. One of the first officers to arrive at the scene of Cregan's crime would later commit suicide and other officers suffered from post-traumatic stress disorder as a result. But there was a huge public outpouring of grief too, and thousands of tributes to Fiona and Nicola poured in, including one from the Queen. We were all overwhelmed at the phenomenal show of public support. Now, however, we had to show everyone that Cregan's crime spree was over – and that we were back in control.

Peter agreed that we should make a statement to the press about the charging together, and so on Sunday afternoon the nation's media piled into Manchester police headquarters to broadcast the statement live. It was the first time I had ever charged someone live on television, but we felt it was important in this instance to amplify our message, to show the country we were working together as a team to bring Cregan and his associates to justice.

A hush descended on the room and the journalists watched us expectantly. I began. I announced that I had authorised the police to charge twenty-nine-year-old Dale Cregan with the murders of two police officers and Mark and David Short, as well as the attempted murder of four other people. I also reminded viewers that now proceedings were active, nothing should be said or reported that could prejudice the trial and jeopardise the courts of justice. Peter added that anyone listening who had information about the murders should look to their consciences and come forward.

Our next step was to prepare for a hugely expensive and high-profile trial, which would cost over £5 million just to police. We hit an obstacle straight away when the courts advised us it wasn't safe to run the trial from Manchester, given the extent and proximity of Cregan's network. Then when we held it instead at Preston Crown Court, the National Offender Management Service wouldn't reclassify Preston Prison as a high-security jail, which was necessary to hold Cregan ahead of the trial. So he had to be kept instead in Strangeways Prison in Manchester and transported to Preston every day in a massive armed convoy, complete with police helicopter, creating something of a media circus. The courtroom was adapted and made bulletproof to protect the judge, witnesses and jury, and scaffolding was erected around the courtroom where armed officers were stationed throughout.

Some 150 officers were involved in guarding Cregan and his co-accused during the trial and dozens of armed officers lined Preston's streets in a lockdown security operation. We had never seen anything like it before, but there were plenty of people who wanted to kill Cregan. We knew many crime gangs in Manchester were angry that he was shining the spotlight on the dark truths of their criminal networks, and they wanted him taken out. But there was no way of penetrating the fortress of security we had created, even if Cregan often came into court whistling the theme tune to *The Great Escape*. He received a whole life sentence, with the Home Secretary giving a guarantee that he would be locked up for the rest of his days.

After the verdict, I struggled with my feelings. Those last few months had represented one of the darkest periods in Greater Manchester Police's history. What was moving, however, was the reaction to the case in the city and beyond. The brutal murders of Fiona and Nicola had touched the public deeply, their deaths stirring powerful emotions and building a groundswell of support for the police. A heightened appreciation of how dangerous their job was and the everyday, heroic bravery of officers was beginning to manifest itself everywhere. Thousands of people lined the streets of Manchester for the funerals of Fiona and Nicola, and police officers from forces across the country travelled to cover shifts so Manchester officers could pay their respects to their fallen colleagues. Over 5,000 people from all walks of life offered to work for free and cover for the police after a #CoverforGMP Twitter campaign had been launched. Highways Agency staff were queuing up to volunteer, train and bus companies were offering to help and grown men and women were struggling to hold back tears.

It was remarkable. We were witnessing something phenomenal, and as I joined some of the community vigils I reflected on the brilliance and bravery of officers in the force. I knew that it would be impossible to do my job without them. And I also knew that this kind of public response was rare: often, the public felt ambivalent about the police. They thought that crime rates were rising, that not enough was being done to keep the streets safe. Or perhaps they felt, like I had witnessed so often before, that justice did not apply to their community. But for now at least, the public were behind the police. When there was a march of honour from Hyde police station, communities from all over Manchester stood together, heads bowed, praying for the two officers in the pouring rain.

This was the opposite of what Cregan had wanted to achieve. He hated the police and yet, through his actions, he was inadvertently building public support for them by the day. Only a year earlier police had been under attack from a thousand people in Salford. They had crouched behind shields and desperately tried to hold their ground as missiles rained down upon them. They had feared for their lives. Now, thousands of people lined the streets of Manchester in an emotional show of support.

In my job you develop an antenna for public confidence. It's that vital, mercurial quality that allows you to get things done. Because when it's gone, everything is an uphill battle. But when it was strong, as it very much was now, it came with true legitimacy – enabling the kind of policing by consent I knew could really make a difference.

A few weeks later, Peter Fahy and I were reflecting on the case, and considering what we might learn from it. Peter had been thinking about how we could get ahead of the criminal networks. One of the frustrating parts of building a case was that government agencies, such as HMRC, only shared information with the police *after* someone had been arrested for something, even though in many cases they already had something that could help make our case. Peter wanted to know if there was a way of changing this. It was the kind of idea I loved – it held such long-term potential.

'This is a once-in-a-lifetime opportunity,' he said, looking me straight in the eye. We knew it was the kind of thing we could only do at a time when public confidence was high.

Peter would write to director generals at the HMRC, Department for Work and Pensions, UK Border Agency, Customs and Excise, the NHS and others, inviting them to meet with the police and Crown Prosecution Service on a regular basis. It was to be a joint venture. We would provide them with a list of people we suspected of being involved in serious criminal activity and they would open their databases to us when it was deemed necessary, providing crucial evidence to help us strengthen our cases. This critical co-operation would mean we could get criminals off the streets before they committed offences, not afterwards.

No one turned down Peter's invitation. How could they? And with that, Operation Challenger was born.

Shortly afterwards, I watched as the directors' glossy cars swung into the car park at Manchester's police HQ for our first meeting of the collected agencies. The Home Office were there to observe and, while we weren't sure how this collaboration would work out, there was an enormous sense of goodwill. We had already provided a list of criminal networks we sought to focus on, and the attendees had brought with them valuable information from their various databases. As everyone got to work, the room was quiet, focused.

There was evidence of fraud and money laundering, HMRC suggested in one case. Substantial benefit fraud too, added the Department for Work and Pensions. He's behind on his VAT payments, chipped in someone else. In next to no time we were able to use this information to build solid cases against dozens of people with known criminal connections, leading to over 400 homes in the area being raided over the next few months as a result, including in Droylsden, Clayton and Tameside, where Cregan had dealt drugs. Criminal gangs there were decimated.

Nearly 350 suspects were arrested, key individuals charged, and around £1 million of illegal drugs and £3 million in property seized by Greater Manchester Police. We had found a new, systemic way of breaking up these criminal networks and, ironically, we had Cregan to thank for it.

The public goodwill wouldn't last forever – it never did. Nothing could. Soon there would be new stories of police failure, new problems to solve. Operation Challenger would begin to flag too, as new priorities surfaced and new targets arrived.

When I think back to Cregan, and that crucial time in Manchester, two things stay with me. The first is Peter Fahy, a leader who I always admired for his approach to policing.

For him, it was about reason, restraint and intelligence. But the job took its toll on him, like it does on all of us. He would eventually stand down, revealing that he had sought counselling to cope with the pressure on his mental health from the strains of the job. His passion and dedication made a lasting impression on me.

The second thing was the feeling of public confidence billowing in our sails, enabling us to finally get one step ahead of the criminals. For a moment, we all felt we had a firm hold on it. It was in our hands and powering us on. Of course, it wouldn't last. But even if it was short-lived, it reminded me that in my job, with the right approach, nothing was ever impossible.

XIII

'What would you say to your younger self?'

It's the question you hear every celebrity asked on television, but I wasn't expecting to hear it myself on a school visit. A small boy, his hand still raised, waited expectantly for my answer. I pictured myself when I was his age. In my mind's eye, I could see myself as a boy. I knew the hopes and dreams of that boy, and I could even feel his heart racing in my own chest. But he suddenly seemed very distant and, for the life of me, I couldn't think of what to say to him. It was then, in the classroom, that I realised: I needed a break.

By the time 2015 arrived, I had prosecuted nearly a million cases. I had worked in the highest courts in the land – quite some journey from my early life in Birmingham – overseeing some of the most notorious cases in British legal history. I had even prosecuted the only case over which Queen Elizabeth II had ever presided, an honour extended to me by the Director of Public Prosecutions in 2002. It was a matter of ceremony to mark the Golden Jubilee so, of course, the Queen wouldn't be making any legal decisions, but it was a moment I thought of with pride. I had been nervous as I entered the Royal Courts of Justice – a fantasy of turrets and towers, spires and pinnacles translated into Victorian reality. Passing through the entrance beneath a giant arch into the Great Hall, it was impossible not to feel the weight of over a century of justice as I crossed the mosaic marble floor, surrounded by soaring arches and elegant stained glass windows ornamented with the coats of arms of Lord Chancellors and Keepers of the Great Seal.

Making my way into the courtroom, I saw that behind me sat every High Court judge in the country, all knights or dames. And then the Queen arrived, along with her husband the Duke of Edinburgh and three judges. They weren't just any judges: they were the Lord Chief Justice, the Vice Chancellor and the Master of the Rolls – the three most senior judges in the land. The Queen and the Duke of Edinburgh took their seats on the raised bench overlooking the court, and I surveyed the courtroom, quite the most spectacular scene I had ever been part of.

I bowed. 'Your Majesty, your Lordships,' I began. 'I am Nazir Afzal, I appear for the Crown, the Respondent in this matter.'

It was a simple Appeal against Sentence imposed by the Crown Court, to be heard by the Court of Appeal, and took only ten minutes, but she watched avidly. When the judges made their decision, the Lord Chief Justice leant over to the Queen, loudly enough for the court to hear.

'What do you think, Your Majesty?'

The Queen laughed, and the rest of the court followed. The judges found in favour of the appellant and reduced the sentence.

'We will rise. This court is adjourned.'

Afterwards, I escaped the drinks reception and stood on the steps outside watching the sun setting over London. These occasions served to remind me how far I had come, but also how different I was to so many at court. Surveying that room of knights and dames, most of them white, most of them from upper-class backgrounds, I thought of my upbringing. That moment came to mind when I sat in the classroom, wondering how to answer the question.

I had never been so close to the heart of the establishment and yet I'd never felt more distant from my profession. I was proud of what I had achieved, of course, and felt blessed to be doing such important work. But I also felt strangely uncomfortable. I had spent a decade being shunned, taken off lists, and excluded from events: I couldn't suddenly feel I'd been welcomed into the bosom of Britain's establishment when I had spent so much time alienated from it. I knew I would never be fully accepted in that company.

That was brought home to me in no uncertain terms a few years later, when I discovered that the Metropolitan Police had been investigating me. The matter had gone on for some time, beginning for me when I was approached by an animated member of the public asking for help at a local authority event

I was attending in Hounslow. The man explained that a friend of his had been threatened by a group of men, one of whom claimed to be Ali Dizaei, then a Borough Commander for the Metropolitan Police and one of the most senior Muslim police officers in Britain. The men had demanded protection money, and threatened to arrest him if he didn't pay up.

I knew of Ali Dizaei, had met him briefly a few times. Some years later he would be jailed for corruption, but earlier in his career he had received compensation from the Metropolitan Police after being wrongly accused of spying for Iran. It was a powerful allegation, and something didn't feel right about it: I pulled up a photograph on my phone and asked whether he was the man who had asked for money.

'No – that's not him.' Someone had been impersonating the officer, and I called him to tell him as much. Having thanked me, he said he couldn't deal with the complaint involving himself, for obvious reasons. A member of his staff would call me, he said. They would eventually find the impersonator and charge him, but it would later transpire that I had been placed under investigation simply because I had warned him of the threat. Of course, I was furious: I had followed the correct procedure, and I was more than a little suspicious that the fact Dizaei and I had brown skin made the Met more likely to look into anything we did.

I told one of the Assistant Commissioners as much.

'Look,' he said, uneasily, 'somebody said that it was inappropriate of you to contact Ali Dizaei when the allegation was *about* Ali Dizaei, so I'm afraid we had no option but to investigate you.'

'Let's get the facts straight,' I responded. 'The allegation was not *about* Ali Dizaei – it was about somebody pretending to be him. And Ali Dizaei was still the police chief for that area.'

'I know, I know,' he said, nervously.

'So why did you start an investigation into me, then, when everyone accepts what I did was right?'

He didn't answer.

'At the very least, I want an apology.'

The next day, I received a letter of apology signed by the Assistant Commissioner.

The case might have been closed, but it stayed with me, a reminder that, as a person of colour, there were always plenty of people watching my every move, waiting for me to slip up. This wasn't just conjecture: a report by Professor Gus John had shown that BAME (black, Asian and minority ethnic) solicitors were much more likely than white solicitors to be subject to investigation by the Solicitors Regulation Authority, and to comprise a higher proportion of those against whom action is taken and are subject to more severe sanctions. In short, you could be investigated for next to nothing and would always be treated differently. I had felt this same prejudice in my own career, particularly when I was chided for being 'too emotive' when I described Stuart Hall as an 'opportunistic predator' after his conviction for sex offences. The case had proven that he was exactly that – a predator – and so when the Lord Chief Justice objected to my words, I wondered whether any other prosecutor would have been subject to the same criticism.

It was one rule for some and another for others, as I saw often. Our justice system is supposedly founded on the principle of equality. Article 7 of the Universal Declaration of Human Rights says that 'All are equal before the law and are entitled without any discrimination to the equal protection of the law.' The reality, which anyone working in the justice system knows, is that there are powerful vested interests working to undermine this. In my more junior career I had seen allegations NFA'd – No Further Action required – when they involved the high-profile or the wealthy, often because a prosecution would not be in the 'public interest'. And I had also seen complainants withdraw their complaints against very wealthy accused, often suspecting that untoward actions – threats, or maybe money – had been employed to make allegations 'go away' before we could prosecute them.

Over time, incidents like this were enough to grind any idealistic prosecutor down. We were supposed to prosecute without fear or favour but in reality we often operated in fear of favours being called in; there was always some powerful figure who could throw a spanner in the wheels of justice. There were also the constraints of officialdom and bureaucracy that, try as I might, I had never quite been able to free myself from, or get used to. There were simply too many times when I felt tethered to a small-minded system. I still had the thirst for justice, but so often the obstacles were exhausting. By the end of my time in the job, I even had to go to a meeting just to get the paper changed for the photocopier.

By the time I came to be sitting in that classroom in 2015, I had been questioning my role for some time. I had monthly meetings with judges, police officers, probation staff, prison authorities and the agenda hardly ever changed: the same cases, the same problems, the progress often negligible. I was a man who needed to feel interested in his work, so it horrified me that it was becoming monotonous. It was the same in court, where you would often feel society's failures: time and time again, the same people came into the courtrooms – and more often than not their children, family and relatives were in the system too. We had an endless cycle of victims and criminals from generations of entrenched poverty, inequality and criminality, and I didn't see that we were doing anything to break it. I was also losing allies, the fellow leaders in the justice system who I felt were kindred spirits. Keir Starmer left to become an MP and Peter Fahy was about to retire.

I had interviewed for the job of Director of Public Prosecutions, but lost out to Alison Saunders. She had a strong career behind her, it was true, but she was very different to me. Maybe I was just a step too far. She was a safe pair of hands in a time of austerity when our budgets were slashed by cuts. I had been forced to cut my staffing numbers by 25 per cent and we'd lost some seriously qualified and capable people as a result. It left a big hole in our skills base and was hurting us. When you are left with 75 per cent of the staff you had before, trying to do 100 per cent of the work – and, let's face it, people are always doing more than their job description anyway, in an overworked institution – something has to give.

Austerity was sucking the life out of the CPS, the bureaucracy was on the increase and it was becoming harder and harder to apply the code for Crown Prosecutors in a creative way. And the justice system itself was coming apart at the seams. For years, we'd seen a criminal justice Bill or new law introduced almost annually. This was the sign that the government was putting a sticking plaster on a bullet wound. What did it mean? It meant that the chances of a fair trial were diminishing by the day. It meant the number of people being prosecuted or handed penalties for crimes was falling to a record low despite the crime rate rising. And it meant that more and more people were walking the streets thinking the same as my dad, when I was growing up in Birmingham: that justice didn't exist.

With morale falling to new lows, I commissioned a company to carry out a one-off survey of my staff. When the results came in, they were even worse than I thought. A sizeable proportion of the team felt work-related stress was getting out of control. Some were even turning to alcohol to try to cope, skipping holidays and working exceptionally – dangerously – long hours to try and get on top of an impossible workload. Reading the report, I felt utterly dejected. Worse, I felt powerless, because I didn't have the budget to change things. I no longer felt like a leader.

We need more staff, Nazir.

'I'm sorry. I can't recruit.'

We haven't had a pay rise in five years.

'I can't give you a pay rise.'

We're working every weekend.

'I'm sorry, I can't give you overtime.'

Can I have a secondment to another department?

'Yes, but I can't replace you because I'm not allowed to bring in anyone else.'

I haven't had a promotion in years.

'I can't give you a promotion. Because there are no vacancies.'

I'd had enough. I was spent. In March 2015 I took early retirement and left the CPS after almost twenty-five years' service. The relief was palpable. That night I got the first eight-hour sleep in years, even though I had no idea what I was going to do next. I just knew I didn't want to be a lifer at the CPS, drained of everything. I wanted that teenage fire back in my belly. People made suggestions for what they thought I should do next. Become a judge, perhaps. There was no way. It was one of the loneliest jobs in the world and, besides, I was happy to see the back of the courtroom.

I decided I would take a little time and feel my way into my new life. I would rediscover my voice, allow myself to be led by my passions. I became an advisor for the Welsh government on issues of violence against women, domestic abuse and sexual violence. I worked with charities, became chair of Hopwood Hall College in Rochdale and started to campaign again on issues I felt passionate about. Now, I was working with international governments, commissions and charities, trying to help with crime prevention.

I was invited to Somaliland to advise on legal reform, where new challenges awaited me. The court hours there ran from 7am to 2pm, which seemed strange. In the streets outside the court, energy seemed to peak at 2pm, so I wondered why it was the end of the working day. As I listened to a cacophony of car horns one afternoon after the court had closed, I asked an official what was going on.

'Don't worry,' he laughed. 'This happens every day. It's the khat delivery.'

I peered through the window and could see people crowded round a truck where bundles of the narcotic plant were being handed out. For the rest of the afternoon nothing happened – and this was why. Work started and finished early so afternoons could be spent chewing khat leaves to achieve *mirqaan*, the Somali word for its euphoric effect.

The legal community there was deeply engaged in its efforts for reform, and I was delighted to be involved in advising their Appeals Court on how cases might be expedited.

Back in the UK, violent offences in England and Wales had risen to their highest level since the National Crime Recording Standard was introduced in 2002. Incredibly, 45 per cent of the public reported having no faith in the justice system, and it was frustrating to see few attempts to address this fundamental issue.

I may have been watching from afar, but it wasn't necessary to be present in court every day to see the problems. All one needed to do was look at the statistics: in 2018, only 8.2 per cent of crimes recorded by police resulted in a suspect being charged or summonsed to court, a pitiful detection rate. The number of people being prosecuted, or sent to jail, has fallen to its lowest in twenty-five years, and there is a backlog of over 32,000 Crown Court cases waiting to be heard while courts sit empty because cuts have decimated staff numbers, meaning fewer sitting days for an already overstretched court. This is what happens when the Ministry of Justice budget is cut by 40 per cent.

The cumulative effect of all this legal chaos is that it normalises crime. There is no effective deterrent, so criminality becomes part of everyday life, particularly when combined with cuts to budgets of other areas like social work, meaning vulnerable communities go unsupported. We can't carry on like this and seriously need to ask ourselves: what is the system for? Some 150 years ago we were all clear that the system was for bringing offenders to justice. We have gone astray.

Take 'diversion', for example, which aims to divert first time offenders away from the criminal justice system to a more appropriate setting to get the support they need so they don't reoffend. This is not compatible with 'revolving door' justice, where the law is making no impact on reoffending rates and criminals keep returning to court, making a mockery of the justice system. We cannot apply the former or tackle the latter when the social infrastructure is being fundamentally dismantled.

I suspect that if members of the public were to go behind the scenes at court, they would be shocked by what they saw. Perhaps this would be a good thing – more transparency would create greater accountability, and perhaps that's what is needed to drive real change. I would love to see cameras in the courtroom streaming what happens in every Magistrates' and Crown Court live on the internet (with appropriate safeguards in place to protect the vulnerable defendants, witnesses and victims, of course).

Time doesn't change things, people do. But it requires bold, imaginative and committed leadership, and the problem is that too many of our leaders are drawn from an ever-shrinking talent pool. Take the police, for example. You have to be at least a Deputy Chief Constable or, in London, Assistant Commissioner to be considered for a Chief Constable role. That means there are around fifty people from whom the leaders for our forty-three police forces can be selected. The pool is so small that it just about covers the vacant positions. After Peter Fahy stepped down, only two people applied for the job of Chief Constable of Greater Manchester Police Force.

Is this really the best way to choose the police leaders we need to tackle the increasingly complex and demanding crime challenges we face? And is it likely to promote the kind of diversity that reflects the communities they serve? So far, it has proven not.

Michael Fuller is still Britain's only ethic minority Chief Constable. He led Kent Police from 2004 to 2010, and since then there has not been another BAME person appointed Chief Constable in the country, and depressingly few in deputy positions either. This problem isn't unique to the police, but it illustrates the problem: our leaders don't look like the communities they serve, nor do they understand them. The status quo is maintained, and nothing changes.

All this leaves us with a combination of catastrophic cuts, a secretive and failing justice system that's losing public confidence, and leaders who don't always deserve their roles.

While I was proud of my work with the CPS, I had always known that a healthy society wasn't just one with a robust justice system: it was one that changed culture and stopped crimes from being committed in the first place. We needed this more than ever in a country that had become angry and polarised, exacerbated by Brexit on the horizon and the resurgence of the far right. Old wounds were reopening across the nation and, in terms of racism, things had become just as bad as when I was a boy on the streets of Birmingham.

With extremism, reactionary populism and nationalism on the rise, society's divisions were manifesting in all sorts of ways. In 2019 I experienced this first hand, after I was asked if I would mediate in a dispute over the teaching of LGBT education in Birmingham schools. The row had started when consultations on the government's new relationships education guidance attracted the attention of religious activists to the school curriculum in Birmingham. Protests started at Parkfield Community School, where the school's gay assistant head-teacher, Andrew Moffat, who had created the No Outsiders teaching programme on inclusivity, was targeted with abuse.

'Shame on Mr Moffat,' an angry man shouted from a mega-phone. 'You are teaching Muslims it is OK to be gay – and it is not.' Various banners were being waved: 'My child, my voice', 'Adam and Eve, not Adam and Steve' and 'My voice must be heard'. The school was forced to stop their No Out-siders lessons, which taught children about different family relationships and the right to equality under the law.

Four other schools in the city also stopped their lessons. But the protesters didn't pack up their placards and mega-phones; they instead redoubled their efforts, beginning to target another school that taught children about same-sex relationships, Anderton Park Primary School. Dozens of activists with megaphones descended on the tiny cul-de-sac in Sparkhill where the school was based. Police stood by and watched, and most ministers remained silent. Where had all this hatred come from?

When Birmingham Council called and asked if I'd mediate, I said I would gladly help. It was shameful to me seeing Muslims from the city where I was born demonstrating such ugly intolerance, intimidating children and shouting abuse.

And when I went through the learning plan about relationship education myself, I realised just how ridiculous the protests were. There were two books that had angered the protesters. One had a picture of two male penguins raising a chick together and the other had a picture of a boy who liked to dress up as a mermaid. There was no sexual content at all.

'Is that it?' I asked the headteacher of the school, Sarah Hewitt-Clarkson. It was shocking that the schools were going unsupported by the Department of Education.

I walked around the school and saw the children skipping around the playground, laughing as they listened to a storyteller, and thriving in the classroom. They shouldn't have to run the gauntlet of hate to get into school every morning.

'I think I need to speak to the activists,' I said. Perhaps we could find some common ground. Surely it couldn't just be those books? When I met the group, however, they assured me it was. As we congregated around a table, I sipped my tea. Their views made no sense to me – especially as many of these activists didn't even have a child at the school – but I knew that to achieve anything, I would need to listen. I agreed to set up a meeting for them with the school, providing they kept up their end of the bargain and cease protesting immediately. For a while it worked, although representatives from the school were quite understandably reluctant to meet with those who had been terrorising them so persistently and aggressively.

But then the situation escalated. The protesters returned, and this time it wasn't just the intimidating presence of surly men, paired with the usual loud torrent of abuse blasted out through megaphones, that we had to worry about. Now, protesters were handing out fake material from the internet, claiming gay sex was being taught at the school.

'Look what they're doing to our children!'

I was losing patience.

'If you want to protest,' I told the activists, 'why don't you protest outside the city council building? You know, where its department for education is based?'

No, they said. They were staying put.

I tried once more.

'How would you feel,' I said, 'if the far right crew were outside this school with megaphones shouting, "we don't want our children to be taught about Islam", "we don't want our children to know Muslims exist". How would you feel about that?'

'That would be wrong,' one of them finally said.

'But it's OK for you to say to the school that gay people can't exist?'

'Yes,' they responded in unison. It was baffling.

'Do you not understand?' I asked. 'My job is to protect your freedoms as much as those of anyone else.'

I paused as I looked at them.

'It's all or nothing. If we don't protect all our freedoms, then we may as well protect none of them.'

But they stayed silent. I had failed to break through. Their eyes had glazed over and in their obstinate expressions, I saw the problems of Britain in 2019 staring back at me.

Everything that was happening here was a microcosm of the wider push-back on equalities taking place across the country and the school inevitably became the focus for all the usual media agitators. Even Katie Hopkins – the same woman who had once said that Islam disgusted her – turned up in Birmingham to support the activists and join them for Eid celebrations. How could we protect our freedoms in such an environment? I was still wrestling with the answer to that question and I was disappointed that my interventions had made little difference, although a High Court judge would eventually ban the school protests. I may no longer be a prosecutor, but as a citizen, I wanted to believe I could still make a difference. Still, I knew what I had always known: keep going, keep trying.

It became frequently less easy to feel positive. Those streets I walked as a child never felt safe to me. Now, they were even more dangerous. On 25 February 2019 at 2pm my brother's nephew, Hazrat Umar, was brutally stabbed to death. He was killed around the corner from where I was born. He was eighteen years old and the third teenager to be killed in the city in twelve days.

Hazrat was on his way to the gym when he was approached by a seventeen-year-old boy with whom he'd had a disagreement over a mobile phone. Hazrat had never been in a gang nor involved in any criminal activity, and was studying as an apprentice. He had everything to live for. But the teenager blocking his way, who was his classmate at South and City College, pulled out a knife. In a totally unprovoked attack, he stabbed Hazrat eighteen times before stamping on his head. Hazrat's killer was captured on CCTV, arrested and pleaded guilty. He was sentenced to life with a minimum term of fourteen years.

When my brother called to tell me the news, I was absolutely devastated. I was numb, heartbroken for him and his wife. I thought about the last time I had seen Hazrat, and of the hopes and dreams shining bright in his young eyes. It took me back to my own teenage self.

I thought again about that question, to which I'd never quite given a satisfactory answer:

What would you say to your younger self?

Well, I would tell him that no matter how maddeningly impossible things may seem at the time, change can happen. You can make a difference, if only you keep hold of what matters. The older you get, the more you need to keep your dreams with you.

Afterword

This book has highlighted many of the failings and successes of the CPS, but as we enter a new decade of criminal justice, it's not just the question of whether we are prepared for the future (we're clearly not) that should be on our minds. It is the question of whether we can continue to rise to the fundamental challenge of why the CPS was established in the first place.

Over thirty years ago, the CPS was created to end miscarriages of justice. Parliament hoped that an independent prosecution service would see the dawning of a new era, with new methods of gathering evidence and prosecuting crimes that would prevent high profile miscarriages of justice such as the Birmingham Six and the Guildford Four, which occurred when the police employed their own prosecutors. Independent oversight, it was hoped, would eliminate miscarriages of justice.

Sadly, though, they do still occur. People still lie, false reports and false witness statements are still made, and police officers still try and hide evidence that undermines their theory of a case. Prosecutors still get some judgments wrong. Yes, there are fewer miscarriages of justice, but the system is not infallible, and grave mistakes are still made.

Every time this happens, it damages public trust in the system that is supposed to protect them. Once an innocent person has been convicted by a jury, the process by which it can be overturned on appeal is slow and convoluted, and it focuses on whether procedures have been followed incorrectly rather than on the bigger question of whether someone might in fact be innocent. The system doesn't seek to determine innocence, it merely looks at process – was the evidence presented in the right way, did the judge sum up correctly? – to establish whether a conviction is 'unsafe'.

If a victim of a false conviction does manage to emerge from the Court of Appeal a free person, they still won't formally be classified as innocent and, because of changes to the law for the wrongly convicted – made by the coalition government – the victim is unlikely to receive any apology or compensation. For many who do manage to overturn their convictions, the years they have spent in prison have caused them to lose everything – and they find themselves homeless, without the support of any family or friends. As it stands, the criminal justice system doesn't recognise whether something is right or wrong – it deals only in procedural grey areas.

This is exactly the problem I encountered in Rochdale. As you have already read, the CPS couldn't bring themselves to admit they had got it wrong, because no one ever says they're wrong in the legal profession. Instead, we cling to that old euphemism, the 'unreasonable', and hope no one notices the failings implied by that word. But without the admission of failure, we will never learn from our mistakes and address the fact that our obsession with process undermines real justice.

There are undoubtedly people in prison who should not be there, as well as many people who should be in prison but have managed to escape justice. I spent most of my career battling with the latter group, the people who were acting with impunity and thought the law didn't apply to them.

But in the last few months of my tenure at the CPS, I found myself looking at case papers that had been sent to me suggesting a miscarriage of justice had occurred. Although it was not my case, the details of the conviction grabbed my attention and it was to be the last case I would explore in detail. This time I wasn't looking to prosecute someone, but to see if we had got it wrong.

Imagine for a moment a small terraced house, where a man lives with his pregnant wife. She doesn't go out unless accompanied by her husband or his relatives, and has no friends that she can call her own.

Despite his wife being pregnant, the man is conducting an affair with a young pharmacist who, upon learning that he is married, decides to call their relationship off. Furthermore, she thinks the man's wife needs to know what kind of man she is married to. So she goes to pay the wife a visit, gets invited in, and has a very emotional conversation. Quite understandably, the wife is deeply unhappy at what she hears.

What follows can be summarised by three facts. First, the wife is found dead shortly afterwards, discovered in a pool of blood. Second, the front door of the house (the only exit to the building) was closed and locked from the inside, so nobody could have left through that door without being let out from someone inside the house. The third and final fact is that the pharmacist drove home via a petrol station where she can be seen on CCTV, wearing the same clothes she left her home in earlier that day. She looks relaxed, and appears to show no signs of having being close to someone who has lost so much blood.

The pharmacist was the only suspect in the murder when this case came to court, and two versions of the story were presented to the jury. The prosecution's explanation relied on the pharmacist stabbing the wife several times. The fatal blow was to her abdomen, where her unborn child lay. As the door was locked, the prosecution argued that to get out of the house, the pharmacist must have climbed on top of a cupboard and then, somehow, through a tiny window. But because there was so much blood, surely in these circumstances one would expect that the pharmacist would have got some of it on her clothes, which would have been found on the cupboard or in that tiny window? That was not the case in this instance.

To explain this missing evidence, the prosecution suggested that the pharmacist had brought along a white paper suit (the kind that forensic scientists wear at crime scenes) and somehow changed into it before killing the wife. No such paper suit was ever found. However, because she was a woman having an affair, the court heard that she must therefore have had a motive to commit this heinous act. Immediately it is clear that the prosecution's case had flaws, yet lawyers will always design an answer to a problem, even if it sounds fanciful in the light of day. It is, after all, their job.

The second version of events was offered by the defence team. Their explanation was that the pharmacist had told the deceased her husband couldn't be trusted, and was subsequently let out of the house by the distressed wife, after which she went home. She didn't commit the murder. Somebody else must have killed the victim, and this could well have been her husband when he returned. This theory had flaws too. Her husband had a reliable alibi that afternoon and the door was still locked from the inside, with the key still in the door inside.

Now it was up to the jury to decide. We often tell people that for a successful murder conviction, the prosecution needs to demonstrate motive, opportunity and means. The question now was who, of the two suggested perpetrators, had more of a motive, opportunity and means?

The jury considered both accounts, and concluded that the pharmacist was guilty. They even asked for the window to be brought into the jury room so see if they could get through the tiny opening. The pharmacist was subsequently convicted and sent to prison for life, still protesting her innocence.

The defence team were not the most dynamic. They lodged an appeal largely on the basis that the judge should not have allowed the jury to carry out their own experiment into the tiny window. This was yet again an appeal based on process, not on whether the convicted woman was actually innocent. The Court of Appeal dismissed the appeal and reaffirmed her life sentence.

Several years passed before a new defence team went to the Criminal Cases Review Commission (CCRC), a body set up to examine potential miscarriages of justice, investigate them and refer them back to the Court of Appeal if necessary.

The problems with the CCRC start with resources; they don't have enough high-quality investigators. Their investigations are poor, in my view, because they take a risk-averse approach, which means they take on only a small number of cases and are perceived as just being gatekeepers for the Court of Appeal rather than champions for the innocent. I wasn't surprised to hear then that after a brief review the CCRC decided they would not refer the case to the Court of Appeal.

Meanwhile, the pharmacist continued to languish in prison for a murder that I was beginning to seriously doubt she had committed. Someone who was in prison with her for a short time had contacted me on her release to say she was deeply concerned that the pharmacist was innocent, and it was this that brought her file to my attention. Having carefully read the case papers, let me offer a third explanation, one which nobody had considered in court.

From the blood pattern analysis report, it is very clear that the deceased would have been sat on the edge of the bed, while bleeding from the cuts to her arms. Crucially, when the deep stab wound to the deceased's abdomen began to bleed, the blood placement indicates the injury was caused while she was sitting and bent over. Therefore at this point she would have been compliant, apparently allowing a third party to kneel in front of her and stab her.

According to experts, the wound to the abdomen would have caused her to fall, which would account for the injury to her forehead above the right eye. Given that abdominal fluid was on the carpet blood pool, she would then have lain bleeding face down for some time. At some point, however, she turned herself (or was turned), as she was lying face up when her sisters and the paramedics arrived.

Blood was on the bedspread and smeared, which would suggest that at some stage she laid on the bed after the injuries were inflicted to her arm and hand, at which point she would have been conscious. Her phone was nearby, so why did she not make a call?

In addition, a total of twenty-one calls and texts were made to the wife by family members between 14:15 and roughly 16:07, when her sisters arrived at the house. Why would there be so many calls and attempts to contact her unless people genuinely thought she might do something to harm herself, or that harm had been brought to her? One sister had called the ambulance saying, 'I think I've just found out my sister's killing herself, killed herself . . . I don't know.'

Crucially, when the paramedics arrived, the pathologist's expert opinion was that the victim was then deceased, within the period to resuscitate. She was still warm, with no signs of rigor mortis or hypostasis. This is strong evidence that would suggest her fatal injuries, the ones to the heart and abdomen, occurred after 14:15 and much closer to when she was found by paramedics at around 16:10.

The pathologist also stated that at least some of the injuries to her 'could have been inflicted by the attacker to mimic self-inflicted injuries'. I am surprised that a pathologist would say this without also suggesting that injuries that *looked* self-inflicted could also look that way because they were *indeed* self-inflicted. In this instance, another possibility arises: that the injuries were self-inflicted, and perhaps made to look like murder to incriminate those who had betrayed her.

With this reading of the evidence, there is a good reason why people contacted me to passionately argue that the pharmacist could be innocent. Both the prosecution and defence advanced flawed arguments and, to me, it seems very likely that the deceased killed herself. A campaign is now underway to get this conviction reviewed and overturned, and I've promised to do everything I can to help the campaign, and the pharmacist.

For me, this case reflects the failings inherent in the system, which happen more frequently than the public might anticipate. The police get a theory and a target suspect, then they find evidence to support it, ignoring any evidence that undermines their theory. Meanwhile, a defence team fails to properly represent their client, and prosecutors, judges and juries make their judgments based on flawed terms, potentially convicting an innocent party.

The announcement that a long-awaited Royal Commission on Criminal Justice will be part of the 2019 government's new legislative programme finally gives us an opportunity to tackle this, and many other critical failings. As the first review of its kind in three decades, it must take an unflinching look at how widespread miscarriages of justice really are. The last Royal Commission of the early 1990s suggested that between 2 and 17 per cent of UK convictions were 'problematic'. How badly do we fare now, I wonder?

Even though I'm no longer working at the CPS, cases are often being brought to my attention. The recent example of Post Office workers from all over the country – mainly subpostmasters – who have been wrongly accused of theft due to accounting failures by the Post Office Horizon IT system is another shameful example. Hundreds were vindicated by a High Court ruling in their favour, showing that the Horizon system caused discrepancies in sub-postmasters' branch accounts. The Post Office will have to pay £58 million in compensation as a result. Yet a number of sub-postmasters had been sent to jail because of such discrepancies and these wrongful convictions destroyed lives, causing some to lose their home and consider suicide.

We cannot wait for another momentous mistaken conviction, such as the Birmingham Six or Guildford Four, before we realise something is going badly wrong.

If the Royal Commission is to do its job properly, it will need to be entirely independent of government and push back against vested interests of the established order that will always resist the real change we need.

There's no point promising a radical overhaul and then only tinkering around the edges. Let's start by asking why so many cases fail? How can we better protect people from being wrongly imprisoned? Why is it that witnesses and victims hate the experience of going to court, to such an extent that many are saying 'never again'? Why would increasing numbers rather turn away if they saw a crime nowadays because they have no faith in the system and don't want to get involved in a failing justice process? Getting genuine answers to these questions would be a strong starting point to overhauling our outdated system. But there's another vital area that needs to be closely examined, and that's leadership culture within the justice system.

We're living in an age where groupthink is growing increasingly dominant across the public sector. We're seeing public servants being restricted in their use of Twitter and leaders increasingly locked in to a beige consensus of blandness. For all the feigned interest in 'diversity', there's no such commitment to diverse thinking. In fact, there is a growing intolerance towards independent voices or those who think creatively and challenge received opinion. Now we have a Prime Minister who boasts that every MP in his party will vote the way he wants, and both of the main political parties are driving genuine thinkers and independent voices out of Parliament. We're left with an increasingly small pool of hand-picked clones who are being pushed forward for the top jobs. And is it any wonder that they get so many of the big decisions wrong?

This is the antithesis of the culture I've tried to build. High-performing, smart teams need a healthy dynamic where challenge is encouraged. 'Tell me if I've got this wrong,' I'd say to my team. 'Tell me if we're going in the wrong direction.' If everyone just nods along then we're not getting to grips with the challenges in front of us, or even thinking properly. We're simply going through the motions, ticking boxes.

I always tried to be an activist-minded prosecutor. Visible leadership, speaking out, pushing restlessly for change and continually trying to improve the system and building a stronger connection with the public – all of these were the things that drove me. While not always enthusiastically embraced, this model was at least accepted at the time. I was always fortunate to have good bosses, who supported me. Nowadays, I fear this is no longer the case.

The process-driven bureaucrats have well and truly taken over. Of course, there are a few notable exceptions, but invisible leadership, say-next-to-nothing minimal engagement and maintaining the status quo are the new watchwords. Hearts and minds aren't there to be won over, they're to be ignored.

Ironically, while leadership in the justice system becomes increasingly cautious and timid, it's the private sector where we're seeing a growth in CEO activism. Corporate leaders are eschewing the cautious approach of their predecessors and passionately advocating for what they think is right on all kinds of issues from the environment to gun control. Interestingly, this reflects changing priorities for business. Edelman's global trust barometer, for example, shows that 69 per cent of CEOs now prioritise building trust as their number one goal, surpassing high-quality products and services. If only the same recognition of the value of trust was felt in the legal system.

The Edelman survey is also a good measure of how leadership expectations are changing. Taking into account the views of over 33,000 respondents across 27 countries, it shows that 76 per cent of people agree that CEOs should take the lead on change rather than waiting for government to impose it. A younger generation coming through wants to see business leaders creating positive change in critical areas such as equal pay, prejudice and discrimination.

But this generation's views and values are not being heard by the legal profession. Clinging to centuries-old traditions in their hermetic bubble, they are impervious to the generational shifts happening elsewhere in the world. If a prosecutor were to speak out now on half the stuff I have been vocal about in my career, they would struggle to get ahead. In fact, they might not remain a prosecutor for very much longer.

When I look at leaders in my field nowadays I can see how the thirst for justice and change is being drained from them. If they step out of line and say something challenging on social media, for example, you won't hear from them again. They will be silenced. This terrifies me because I know nothing will get better if our leaders are weakened in this way. Change happens when leaders are empowered, not cowed.

Not long ago I sat before a group of police leaders making the case for a different data-sharing approach, with the aim of making the public feel safer and reducing violent crime. It would be a pioneering but entirely manageable step forward. But before I had even finished making my case, I could see in the nervous glances being shared across the room, the fears of a risk-averse culture starting to awaken.

'We've never done this. I don't think we can do that,' someone said.

A series of half-hearted excuses followed, as I tried to get those present to focus on the bigger picture. But no one was listening. How could I get them to swim to new horizons when they didn't have the courage to lose sight of the shore? I've had similar conversations with leaders in my field when they've complained about appalling processes that have been forced upon them. I always encourage them to speak up, and to challenge bad decisions.

'I can't do that. There will be consequences,' they say.

And that, more than anything, is what's holding us back. I write this at a moment in history when Britain's criminal justice system is broken. The stakes could not be higher. While government promises a genuine, wide-ranging reform and dramatic improvement, none of this will happen. Not until we trust leaders to make good decisions and cut the leash.

It remains an honour and a privilege that so many victims, survivors and groups that work with vulnerable people all over the world have put their trust in me. It is to them that I commit what's left of my life. Not just in the patron or ambassador roles I am thrilled to hold, but as an activist on their behalf. I look at the poverty of ambition in governments and agencies and promise to hold them to account for their failures, as a critical friend who wants to see them improve.

I cry when I see poverty, abuse and despair, as do so many others. I want to stop the tears. I am often asked how, having seen humanity at its worst, am I able to remain positive. It's simple: I have hope in the power of the individual. Each one of us has it in them to save lives. In the days I have left, I intend to save more.

Epilogue

November 2020

At the turn of the millennium, we might have felt that we were starting to leave the injustices of the last century behind. But in recent years these hard-won gains began to slip through our fingers. Nothing, however, could prepare us for 2020, the year when everything *really* began to unravel. As Covid-19 ripped through the UK, it felt as though the pandemic was pulling at an invisible loose thread. Stitch by stitch, the justice system began to come apart at the seams. It became overwhelmed by a backlog that has continued to grow every week since the start of lockdown, and shows no signs of abating.

As I write this, over half a million criminal cases are waiting to be dealt with by the courts. Victims will have to wait years for justice to be delivered and, for those defendants left languishing in custody, some will have served longer on remand than they would have been sentenced to if convicted by the time their case comes to trial.

This is a monumental failure of justice and carries a heavy human cost. Long delays not only cause continued pain and, in some cases, the total collapse of trials. They also see public confidence, and trust in the system, drain away. The slower the wheels of justice turn, the less likely they are to ever reach their destination. Officers retire, witnesses forget, and cases go nowhere. Worse still, as trust in the system disappears, people lose hope in the very idea of justice. The Victims' Commissioner Dame Vera Baird has warned of increasing numbers 'giving up on justice and walking away'. I fear she's right.

But it isn't just advances in social justice that have been lost during the pandemic. As scenes of patients and medical professionals in dire straits were beamed into our living rooms on the news, showing a health service pushed to its limits, it quickly became apparent that many lives would be lost. The pandemic didn't discriminate: it took tens of thousands of lives at will. Waves of grief followed its path – and I was not immune to its random cruelty.

On 8 April I took a call no one ever wants to receive. I was told my older brother Umar had died. The next day we found he had tested positive for Covid-19: the cruel disease that has defined 2020 had taken his life.

I knew he had been ill, but he had told me he was getting better and assured me there was no need to visit. He was the fittest in our family and, we thought, was stronger than us all, so there was every reason to believe him. When I got the call I felt numb with shock, and even now I still find it hard to accept he is gone.

Umar had supported me all his life. While I was at the

library and all my brothers were working in the family business, it was Umar who defended me, telling my brothers to let me study and follow my own career path. He was always proud of everything I achieved and, when he eventually got to work in the courts, providing translation services for the Home Office and the police, he proudly told everyone that he was my brother.

And I was enormously proud to see him there too. He spoke half a dozen languages from the subcontinent and was never fazed by anything. And he was a kind, decent man: no one ever fell out with Umar. He was such a calming influence on our family and Mum adored him, her first born. For as long as I could remember she had prayed every day that she would die before her children, and so I knew that the loss would be devastating for her. She was also seriously ill at the time of his death, and a few months later she passed away. I believe that she died of a broken heart.

The weeks that followed were among the toughest of my life. I drove to my brother's house to meet my family. We were given gloves and masks and went upstairs to carry Umar's body down. Because it was the undertaker's policy not to enter the house during lockdown, we had to put him in a body bag and on a stretcher ourselves. Before we handed him over, Mum – who was outside and was herself attached to an oxygen tank – asked if she could see her son for the last time. We zipped open the body bag just enough to show her his face through the window. It was absolutely heartbreaking.

Umar's wish was to be buried in Pakistan with my father but this was impossible because there were no flights. It wasn't going to be straightforward finding a burial plot in Birmingham either. We were advised by the coroner that they had a 300-body backlog and wouldn't be able to get a death certificate for us until the following week.

The undertaker had another 14 bodies to pick up that day and told us there was no space in their morgue for my brother. So arrangements were made with a private undertaker, and in the meantime Umar was kept in a mortuary fridge. When we were eventually able to bury him nine days later, I wasn't able to go to his funeral as only six people could attend; our family was too large to allow everyone to be with him as he was buried. My brothers and his son lowered Umar's body into the ground and after 29 minutes they were told to leave the area, as the next family had arrived to bury their loved one.

It was all so cold, so rushed and inhumane. We couldn't grieve together as a family. But, as painful as it felt, we accepted these conditions. Families everywhere were having to make extraordinary sacrifices as part of the lockdown. People had been shielding at home for months, not able to work or even get a hug from their loved ones. We did it because we obeyed the law, and because we wanted to protect others.

It was during this time, while I was trying to come to terms with my loss, that I saw reports of the Prime Minister's special adviser Dominic Cummings travelling up and down the country. He journeyed up to Durham on 27 March and, we now know, was going on a day trip to Barnard Castle on his wife's birthday while in Birmingham we were waiting to get a death certificate to bury my brother.

At the time there was strong national support for the government and its lockdown measures, as people generally recognised we were facing a national crisis and everyone had to pull together. There had been other public figures who had broken lockdown rules, but they had resigned when caught. But when it came to the Cummings affair, support in the government quickly began to collapse as ministers scrambled to try and defend what I considered to be the indefensible. The sole priority, it seemed to me, was to keep a man in his job after breaking regulations that he himself had helped to formulate.

The unedifying spectacle continued, with Cummings holding a Rose Garden press conference at Downing Street to justify his actions – something he should not have been afforded as a civil servant. Staring into the cameras and somehow managing to keep a straight face, he claimed he'd made a trip to Barnard Castle to test his eyesight.

Cummings' apparently flagrant disregard of lockdown regulations was, in my view, to represent a turning point. The public could see he was taking us all for fools, and attitudes and behaviours started to dramatically change as a result. Research published in the Lancet would later confirm this and Durham's former chief constable said Cummings' reported behaviour had made it harder for officers to enforce the rules. One tabloid newspaper even printed a free Dominic

Cummings mask on its front page. 'Can't be bothered with sticking to the rules like the rest of us? Simply wear our handy Dominic Cummings face mask'.

The mockery, however, missed the bigger point. Without public trust in the government's ability to manage the pandemic, many, many more people like my brother were going to lose their lives.

Much of this book has been about trust. It's the glue that binds society together. It's how representative democracy works. Confucius once famously said that three things are needed for government: weapons, food and trust. If a ruler can't hold on to all three, they should give up the weapons first and the food next. Trust should be guarded and maintained to the very end, as without trust we cannot stand. This much was obvious to me: one man was recklessly throwing it away, and as a result we had a government on its knees at a time of national crisis.

It was disturbing to watch. The UK had the highest levels of excess deaths in Europe and our efforts to contain Covid-19 were pitifully inadequate. Ministers had rushed to shield an unelected advisor while leaving care homes dangerously exposed.

I've spent a lifetime thinking no one was above the law and I knew then that if I was still a prosecutor I would have been looking at whether there was sufficient evidence to bring a case against Cummings. If those in power can't be held accountable, then the law is meaningless.

As soon as I made it publicly known that I wished to get to the bottom of this debacle, witnesses began to get in touch with new information. We raised enough money through crowdfunding to instruct solicitors and gather evidence of what we believe are lockdown rules being broken. Within months I was able to submit a 225-page dossier to the Crown Prosecution Service, alleging that Cummings was responsible for six breaches of lockdown regulations. We believed the evidence was there to prosecute and that the public interest test was also met, especially given the impact that his behaviour had on public compliance with Covid-19 rules.

However, as I am no longer part of the Crown Prosecution Service, I have no idea what it will do with this evidence. What kind of Crown Prosecution Service would review the dossier? Was it one that honoured its first responsibility to the public, which prosecuted without fear or favour, and was robust and transparent? Or one that may feel constrained by the establishment, worried about how its actions would be perceived?

We await their decision.

It feels to me there was a time when being British meant you respected, and followed, certain codes of conduct. If you failed, you resigned. If you lied to Parliament, you resigned. But that no longer seemed to be the case. There was no honour anymore. We found ourselves in a Trumpian post-truth, post-shame era, where politicians did everything for power at the expense of legitimacy.

Meanwhile, injustices were emerging everywhere. Domestic violence cases surged during lockdown. Shocking conditions in garment factories in Leicester were exposed, with a retail giant accused of modern slavery after it emerged workers were paid below minimum wage and forced to work long hours in unsafe conditions. And ministers were accused of having 'baked in' educational inequality, as children from poorer backgrounds had their A level results unfairly downgraded by a government computer algorithm.

The problem of powerful sexual abusers hasn't gone away either. In a year in which Hollywood mogul Harvey Weinstein was sentenced to 23 years in prison for rape and sexual assault, the #MeToo movement was still very much alive. But sadly our justice system failed to keep up. Rape convictions in the UK fell to such a record low in 2020 that rape was effectively decriminalised.

The growing gap between law and justice was matched only by an increasing sense of anger. Covid-19 was exacerbating inequalities, and resentment was building – and not just in the UK. In the USA, where the pandemic had been handled even more poorly by the government, one heinous act on the streets of Minneapolis would trigger a global movement.

On 25 May police officers arrested a 46-year-old black man called George Floyd on suspicion of using a counterfeit $20 bill. Floyd was handcuffed and pinned to the ground. A white police officer then forced his knee down on Floyd's neck for over eight minutes. During this time, witnesses shouted at the officer to stop and recorded disturbing footage, later shared on social media, of Floyd begging for mercy and gasping that he couldn't breathe. In his last moments he pleaded for his mother before slipping into unconsciousness.

Minutes later, the officer finally removed his knee from the prone Floyd, who was subsequently taken to Hennepin County Medical Centre where he was pronounced dead.

The footage of his brutal killing shocked the world and went viral, immediately becoming a rallying cry for change, sparking international protests. The Black Lives Matter movement showed there was only so much injustice people can stand before an uprising erupts.

Statues of confederate soldiers were torn down and the conversation around racism changed overnight, including in the UK where statues of slave owners were also toppled.

Covid-19 may have brought the world to a standstill and caused unbearable suffering to so many, but it also achieved something that wouldn't have happened in more 'normal' circumstances: it forced the world to slow down, and made us stop and see things afresh. Our institutions may have been failing to deliver justice, but that didn't mean the public's appetite for it had diminished. In fact, in the 'new normal' people hungered for it even more, seeking news ways to redress the balance.

New leaders sprung up from many unexpected places, and Greta Thunberg observed that 'people are starting to find their voice, to sort of understand that they can actually have an impact.'

In Manchester I watched with awe as a 22-year-old Manchester United footballer began an incredible campaign to feed hungry children. Drawing on his own experiences growing up in difficult circumstances, Marcus Rashford won huge public support as he mobilised hundreds of businesses and councils to provide food parcels to families that needed them. He also forced the Government not once but twice to u-turns on free school meal commitments and pledge hundreds of millions of pounds to supporting vulnerable families. It was a stunning success and remarkable example of a young leader speaking a powerful truth about poverty. 'This system was not built for families like mine to succeed,' he argued, 'no matter how hard we are working.'

Rashford was alive to something that our leaders had failed to notice. Before the pandemic, a UNICEF report showed that 10 per cent of children in the UK were living in households affected by 'severe food insecurity', poverty that results in hunger. During lockdown this became worse as people lost their jobs.

'This is not politics, this is humanity,' Rashford said. 'These children matter. These children are the future of this country. They are not just another statistic. And for as long they don't have a voice, they will have mine.'

As a prosecutor I had spent my career fighting to give a voice to those invisible members of society. It was how I defined leadership – and here was a young footballer stepping up to do the same in an incredibly powerful way, with such eloquence. It was a sign that while our politicians and failing institutions could turn a blind eye to inherent unfairness, a new generation wouldn't do the same – and I drew great inspiration from that.

From the growth of sustainable fashion, which takes into account the environmental and social impact of production, to the Build Back Better movement, activism during the pandemic continued to amplify the fight for social justice.

And that's the thing about justice. It can seem to sleep for a long time, appearing virtually moribund. But then, when least expected, it awakes. And while I write this at a time when our enfeebled justice system is at its lowest ebb, jeopardising the rights of individuals and shredding our social fabric in the process, I am optimistic that better times are ahead – and that a new generation will insist on rebuilding a justice system that we can be proud of.

It can't happen soon enough.

Acknowledgements

As the son of immigrants, I owe a huge debt to my parents. They bravely left their home and all that was familiar to come to an alien country simply because they wanted me and my siblings to have a better life than theirs. They saw war, the horrors of Partition, the death of loved ones – but still thought only of their children.

Writing about yourself isn't easy, I have been on a journey of rediscovery that I am privileged to share with you. I always reminded myself and my various audiences that I was the public's servant. They had entrusted me with responsibility and I had to repay their trust. I often felt that contract keenly, but never more so than through the thousands of victims and survivors who put their lives in my hands. They honoured me with their faith. They shamed me with their courage. It is to each one of them that I offer my gratitude. Their lives immeasurably improved mine.

To that survivor who told me her recovery from decades long trauma only began when I believed her, you will never know the impact you had – you changed me. You taught me that we must refuse to just be born, die, and leave no sign that we were here.

This book would simply not have happened without my co-writer Matt Baker. He has helped me recall memories that I had discarded and then guided me as we turned them into the words on these pages. My editor Robyn Drury has, with her immense professionalism and support, brought this book to you. Her team at Ebury, Penguin Random House made this look all so easy, when it clearly was not. Thank you all.

Nothing I ever did was possible without the extraordinary colleagues in policing and justice with whom I worked. They lived by my side for decades and fulfilled my every hope and desire. We delivered Justice together, and I remain in awe of their knowledge and commitment.

Above all, I must thank my family. I took so few days off when my children were young that I do not blame them for not recognising my contribution to their lives back then. They, however, have always enhanced mine. Through thick and thin, they kept me sane when events were threatening to drag me in a different direction. When people came for me, when others attacked me, tried to belittle me, my family picked me up and dusted me down. My words are inadequate to convey my joy at having them with me. I love them all with every breath I take.

Finally, I want to thank the army of volunteers who work tirelessly, at great personal cost, to protect and support victims and survivors who truly have nobody else. It is shameful that they have to do so whilst operating on a shoestring. It has been a privilege to work with them and for some of the most vulnerable people in this country. You moved me with your honesty, you touched me with your determination and drove me on when I was flagging. You are the best this country has to offer.